CONNECTED
CLOSENESS TO CHRIST THROUGH BIBLE STUDY

CONNECTED
CLOSENESS TO CHRIST THROUGH BIBLE STUDY

Scripture taken from the NEW AMERICAN STANDARD BIBLE, copyright 1960, 1962, 1963, 1968, 1971, 1972, 1973, 1975, 1977 by the Lockman Foundation. Used by permission.

© Copyright 2018

Cover Designer: Steven Smith: designbysteven.com

ISBN: 978-1-7326385-0-1

No part of this book may be reproduced without written permission, except for brief quotations in books, articles, and critical reviews.

Dedicated to

My wife, Gayle, and kids, Rylan and Caitlyn, who display all the greatest attributes of family, faith, and friendship,
And to all my students through the years, whose questions and observations have provided the fuel for this book.

Contents

1: Why Study the Bible? 13

2: Study is Worship 23

3: Prerequisites to Bible Study 33

4: Study the Book 51

5: Completing a Topical Study 91

6: Applying God's Word 105

7: What's Next? 117

Introduction

The study of the Bible is a monumental task. Not only because of the enormous amount of information, or the complexity of that information, but also because the information found in Scripture is randomly formatted. In other words, we cannot go to a section of the Bible and find all the information about a particular topic. To understand a subject like sin, for example, we need to study passages throughout Scripture. Even though one passage might be more informative than others, a complete understanding cannot be achieved until we know what the entire Bible has to say about it.

Knowing this, we can facilitate our study by first organizing the Bible into a format that makes it easy to categorize the information we acquire from it. Theology is an effective way of accomplishing this. It is an "organizational chart" that effectively puts Biblical information in an understandable form. We will not deal with theology here. Our focus is on getting the information from the Bible and learning how to apply it. The process of retrieving information will build a relationship between you and the Lord, and while the information in Scripture is important, it is the relationship that grows from the process of finding the information that we seek.

Relationships are built when people engage in a process that causes them to grow closer to each other. These relationships can be professional or personal. In either case, getting to know and understand each other enhances the relationship. It improves trust and understanding, and it allows the partners to rely on each other. Each has a role in the relationship and should be trusted to perform their roles well.

This is a main characteristic of friendships: trust. Friends usually trust each other, they usually care about each other, and they will usually make sacrifices for each other. But how do they get to that level. How do friendships begin and how do they grow? There are certainly more than a few factors that determine this, but the one we will concern ourselves with is communication.

No person who met someone they were interested in would try to build a relationship with them by using an intermediary. In other words, you wouldn't get to know your future wife by sending her messages through your friend. Telling her how beautiful she looks and how wonderful she is and how much you enjoy her company are messages that need to come directly from you without the use of a messenger. Otherwise, she may end up falling in love with the messenger. Communication is essential when developing relationships, but this communication needs to be personal and intimate. This is true of marriages, friendships, business relationships, or any other type of relationship. Knowing *about* a person is easily accomplished. You can hear about them from other people, read about them in books and newspapers, or learn about them from television. You can even interview them or listen to them speak at a seminar and learn a lot about them. But you won't *know* them. You can know about any celebrity by reading his autobiography or his news clippings, but you won't know him the way his son, or nephew, or neighbor, or co-worker would. You certainly wouldn't know him the way his wife would.

Many of us get to know *about* God, but we never get to *know* God. We learn all we can from pastors' sermons, commentaries, radio programs, and books that are written on a variety of Christian topics. But we never make the effort to know God by interacting with Him directly. Those other sources are messengers, and it is easy to fall in love with them. I'm sure you know someone who knows a lot about God but seems to be in love with their collection of commentaries or other books. You may also know of people who are in love with certain teachers. They seem to have formed an allegiance to them. They'll go to extraordinary lengths to see or hear them speak. They know more about the one who gives them information about God than they know God.

The information we get from others about God can be retrieved from God Himself without the use of an intermediary. We *can* have a personal relationship with God. We don't need to feed off someone else's relationship.

This is the whole point of Bible study. God speaks to us through His Word, the Scriptures. We speak to Him through prayer. This two-way communication is how we build our relationship with Him. We won't study prayer here; our focus will be on learning to hear from God by understanding how to study His Word, and the objective of that study is not solely the acquisition of information, but primarily the development of relationship.

Gathering information is essential to building relationships, but it is not the goal of relationships. Learning about God, from God, is the first step in building relationship. Ultimately, we need to begin to be like Him too. The process of gathering information and assimilating it begins the relationship process, but the process will die if the knowledge we acquire goes unused. The goal of relationship is transformation. When a husband and wife marry, they begin the process of cleaving to each other. They become one flesh. To achieve this, they must change, or transform. Their relationship will also transform. It will grow deeper and more intimate. This happens because the couple learns more about each other and dedicates themselves to applying what they learn. A relationship with God is similar to the husband-wife relationship. He does not transform, but learning more about Him should cause us to transform. But the transformation, like the husband-wife relationship, will only happen if we apply what we learn.

Getting information from Scripture is the beginning of relationship, transformation through application of what we learn is the result of relationship. This book is designed to show how this process of studying Scripture can help us become and remain connected to Christ through Bible study.

With all of that being said, this book is designed to be very fundamental. I usually encourage my students to take other Bible study courses because there are different methods and motivations to study the Scripture. We will talk very briefly about some of these in Chapter One.

In any college curriculum, there are different levels of most subjects. The freshman begins with Chemistry 101, for example, and the sophomore advances to Chemistry 201, and so on until the Chemistry requirement has been met. This Bible study book is designed to be more basic than the 101 level course. If this book were to be used as a textbook for a course, it would be for Bible Study Methods 001.

Why? Because every Christian knows, or should know, the importance of studying God's Word. Many will read the Bible, but not study it. They put more effort into studying school textbooks than they will Scripture. There are different reasons for this, but the solution for all these reasons is simple. If the average Christian understood that it is possible to get information about God directly from God, they would be more motivated to study. Once the student realizes that they do not need to rely solely on sermons and books written by preachers and teachers and that they can build a relationship with God on their own, they will be motivated by their increasing relationship to keep studying. Just like getting a response from the girl that the persistent guy pursues will motivate him to continue his pursuit, so the Christian who hears from God daily will be motivated to continue their pursuit of Him through the study of His Word. That motivation should propel the Christian toward a deeper walk with Christ, and the desire to continually deepen that walk will lead to a more advanced level of Bible study, provided by the more advanced courses mentioned earlier.

That motivation to pursue God through the relationship that is built by Bible study is the point of this book. It is not designed to be an advanced treatise of all the tools and methods used to study the Bible. It is instead designed to motivate the student to go deeper. Prayerfully, this will lead them from Bible Study 001 to Bible Study 101, and then into Bible Study 201, and on, and on.

My prayer is that this book accomplishes this goal for the Glory of God and to the advancement of His Kingdom.

1: Why Study the Bible?

Few Christians would deny the importance of studying the Bible, but if asked the reason for their study, the answers would vary. The desire to study Scripture is shared among believers, but the motivations differ. The environments in which each Christian is taught will have a large impact upon the reason they study. Some will simply seek knowledge, while others are motivated to defend their faith against opposition.

What does Scripture teach about studying. What is the biblical reason for delving into God's Word? What is the goal of study? What results should we hope to achieve? The Bible gives answers to these questions, and the Christian who has a desire to study Scripture should use the biblical reasons for their study to examine their motivations. In this chapter, we will examine a few of these reasons.

Knowledge and Growth

In his epistle, Peter writes:

> as also in some of his letters, speaking in them of these things, in which are some things hard to understand, which the untaught and unstable distort, as they do also the rest of the scriptures, to their own destruction.
>
> You therefore, beloved, knowing this beforehand, be on your guard lest, being carried away by the error of unprincipled men, you will fall from your own steadfastness,
>
> but grow in the grace and knowledge of our Lord and Savior Jesus Christ.

2 Pet. 3:16-18a

Peter refers to men who, instead of studying to gain an understanding of the scriptures, distort them. He describes them as untaught, meaning they did not take the time to receive instruction, either through self-study or formal training. As a result, they became unstable in their understanding of the Word.

The difficulty in understanding Scripture was enough of a deterrent to keep them from making a genuine effort to gain knowledge. The resulting lack of knowledge led to their instability. Peter is concerned that his audience will be led astray by men like these and his remedy for them is to grow in the grace and knowledge of our Lord Jesus Christ.

He warns his readers to be on guard against the unstable; but how will they know who is teaching the scriptures correctly and who is distorting them? The answer is that by growing in knowledge, they will be able to discern error when it is being taught.

There are two words for knowledge in the New Testament: *epignosis* and *gnosis*. Both words mean knowledge, but *epignosis* is the type of knowledge that is acquired through experience. We will discuss this type of knowledge in more detail later, but it is the difference between knowing a stove is hot because your parents said so and knowing it is hot because you touched it. Hearing it from your parents is *gnosis*. Touching the stove is *epignosis*. There are two ways to learn the stove is hot. Verbal instruction (*gnosis*), and experience (*epignosis*).

The word Peter uses in this passage is *gnosis*. He is admonishing his readers to learn the scriptures through academic study so that they will increase in knowledge and improve their ability to discern error.

In chapter 1 of the same epistle, Peter writes:

> 12 Therefore I shall always be ready to remind you of these things, even though you already know them, and have been established in the truth which is present with you.
>
> 13 And I consider it right, as long as I am in this earthly dwelling, to stir you up by way of reminder,
>
> 14 knowing that the laying aside of my earthly dwelling is imminent, as our Lord Jesus Christ has made clear to me.

> 15 And I will also be diligent that at any time after my departure you may be able to call these things to mind.

His concern was that his readers would know what they believed. Understanding the truth of Scripture helps the Christian apply it more easily. It also helps fend off false teaching. The world was blossoming with all types of heresy in Peter's day. Some of it was foreign to the church; it originated from religions and cultures that the Church was only beginning to discover. Other heresy came out of the Church by false teachers who everyone thought were sincere, but turned out to be wolves in sheep's clothing. Developing a good academic knowledge of Scripture helped to keep the believer safe from the influence of false teaching.

There is, however, a more thorough type of knowledge.

Paul writes in Colossians chapter 1:

> 9 For this reason also, since the day we heard of it, we have not ceased to pray for you and to ask that you may be filled with the knowledge of His will in all spiritual wisdom and understanding,
> 10 so that you may walk in a manner worthy of the Lord, to please Him in all respects, bearing fruit in every good work and increasing in the knowledge of God;

> 11 strengthened with all power, according to His glorious might, for the attaining of all steadfastness and patience; joyously
>
> 12 giving thanks to the Father, who has qualified us to share in the inheritance of the saints in light.

The word for knowledge in this passage is *epignosis*. We mentioned earlier that this word means to learn about something by experiencing it. It's the difference between knowing how to hit a baseball because you watched all the popular instructional videos and knowing how to hit by getting in the batter's box and practicing. Paul is writing to Christians in a city that had been infiltrated with Gnosticism, which is a religion that worshiped knowledge. Their basic tenet was that knowledge sets a person free and enables him to shed his humanity, which is sinful. Matter was evil. Thought, or the immaterial part of man, contained the key to salvation. Two factions developed from this belief. The first believed the body was worthless and useless and it had to be kept in check. The solution to this problem was severely disciplining the body by not indulging in any physical or sensual pleasures. Normal bodily appetites had to be suppressed. The other faction also considered the body evil, so they reasoned that it was useless to restrain it. Their solution was to allow the body to do anything it wanted, so they indulged in all sorts of deviant behaviors. They thought that since the body was evil, they should not try to save it. Instead they should allow it to follow its natural path.

Paul lets the church know that his prayer is for them to acquire knowledge by experiencing God instead of learning about Him through pure academic pursuit. The knowledge they needed was not man made, nor was it intuitive. They needed to learn about God from God Himself and not from any human source. As we mentioned earlier, the way to get this knowledge is through the study of the Word and prayer. The best way to get to know someone is to talk to them, and the way we communicate with God is through Bible study and prayer.

Paul continues by listing some of the effects a believer should expect to receive from communing with God. Walking in a manner worthy of Him, being able to please Him and bear fruit, growing closer, being endowed with the strength to be steadfast and patient, and becoming joyous and thankful are all benefits of a relationship with God which is built through Bible study.

Some of the Colossian Christians had left the faith because of the Gnostic influence. Paul explained that true relationship with God would develop a closeness that would bring the growth and benefits listed above. Paul mentioned in verse 9 that the Colossians should be filled with knowledge, and in verse 10 he says they should increase in knowledge. What he means is that the relationship grows closer and closer as God is experienced at an increasing level. This closeness strengthens and motivates the Christian in such a way that it enables us to repel erroneous teachings and philosophies, like Gnosticism. It also motivates us to live righteously and in a manner that pleases God.

Peter makes it clear that academic knowledge is necessary for the Christian so that we will be aware of the teachings that form our faith. But Paul instructs us that while academics are important, experience is better. It brings benefits that purely academic knowledge does not. I have known several seminary graduates who have talked about how the course load is so heavy that they are forced to study the Word purely for informational purposes. This increases their knowledge of the Bible, but not necessarily their knowledge of their Savior. They develop *gnosis*, at the expense of *epignosis*. They talk about how their faith and relationship to Christ becomes lifeless and dry. They know more than they ever have, but they also care less than they ever have. Getting to know God by experiencing Him prevents a dry, lifeless, careless existence for the Christian.

Please understand that I am not trying to paint all seminarians as dry, lifeless Christians who only care about racking up knowledge. I only wish to point out the potential dangers of study habits that are primarily for gathering information.

Scripture teaches that academic knowledge, or *gnosis*, can help us know how to live righteously, but relationship, or *epignosis*, can give us the motivation, strength, and enablement to live righteously. For this reason, relationship is the primary reason Scripture gives for our study of the Word.

Relationship

Why is relationship so important? How does it give us strength that pure knowledge does not. A popular proverb declares that "knowing is half the battle". But the other half is doing. It is one thing for a football player to know his plays, but it is another thing to be able to execute his responsibility on each of those plays. Knowing the play is only half the battle; being able to block the opponent, or catch the pass is the other half.

For the Christian, the ability to do what we are called to do is as important as knowing what to do; but after we understand what we are called to do, how do we get the ability to actually do it? In his gospel, John describes a level of intimacy with our Savior that empowers us to live according to our potential by tapping into His power and not relying on our own efforts.

In John 15:4-10, John talks about abiding with Christ. This subject is so important that he mentions the word *abide* ten times in this passage. The Greek word for abide is *meno*, and it means to remain or to dwell. He speaks about abiding with Christ the same way a branch abides in the vine. The vine brings nourishment to the branch which helps it build strength. The branch, in turn, produces fruit, which is its reason for existing. As long as the branch remains connected to the vine it can fulfill its calling. Why? Because the nutrition the branch needs to grow strong and produce fruit is routed through the vine. If there is no connection, there will be no strength. The only way for the branch to have the strength to fulfill its mission is to stay connected to the vine.

John lists four benefits to abiding in this passage. The first is productivity. John speaks in verses 5 and 6 of the connected Christian bearing fruit for the Kingdom. Any of us who would like to see our efforts for God's Kingdom be more dynamic can be sure that maintaining our connection to Christ will produce that result.

The second benefit John mentions is inclusion. In verse 6 he says that those who become disconnected will be thrown away. The natural assumption is that those who remain connected to the vine, which is Christ, will be included and will reap the rewards of living in the Kingdom.

Next, John talks about answered prayer. The promise is that those who remain in Christ can ask whatever they will and be confident that their requests will be granted. Of course someone who is connected to the vine will probably not ask for something that is incongruent with God's will. The psalmist explains this when he says that the person who delights himself in the Lord will have the desires of his heart met (Psalm 37:4). This does not mean that God will give you everything you want. It simply means that He will modify your desires so that they match His. Therefore, John could say that whatever you ask will be granted because he knows that you will only ask for what God wants you to have anyway.

The final benefit is relationship. The promise is that the love shared between the Father and His Son will be extended to anyone who is connected to the vine. The love mentioned here is *agapeo*; it is the sacrificial love Christ displayed in His death, and currently displays in His life. It leads us to consider others before we think about ourselves. Their needs take priority over ours.

The end result of abiding with Christ will be transformation. Just like a grape that has remained connected to the vine grows from a bud on the vine into a mature fruit, so will a baby Christian grow from infancy to maturity as long as he is connected to Christ. And just as a mature, plump grape is more useful than an immature grape, so is a mature and well-developed Christian more useful to God's Kingdom than an immature babe.

What could be the goal of relationship? Primarily, to experience the love of God and His Son. Both passages in Colossians and John that we discussed speak about knowing God by experience rather than just knowing about Him intellectually.

Another goal of relationship is to acquire His strength. Again, both passages discuss this. Colossians talks about being strengthened with the ability to be steadfast, patient, joyous, and thankful. The final goal of relationship is to be able to do His will. The relationship provides both the motivation and the ability to bear the fruit that is demanded of us. We are not capable of bearing fruit for the Kingdom of God unless we abide in Him and draw strength directly from Him.

While there is more than one reason to study Scripture, relationship is the reason that results in intimacy and power. It is what compels us to live for God's kingdom, and it empowers us to bear the fruit that is required. Studying the Bible should not be a purely academic process. Our desire and goal should be to grow closer to the Risen King by experiencing His love.

2: STUDY IS WORSHIP

When you decide to delve into God's Word, you are making a decision to worship Him. In order to talk to Him and hear Him instructing you, you will need to be equipped to get into and remain in His presence. Whenever you bow to pray, you are talking to God, and when you talk to Him, you will be in His presence. In the same way, when He talks to you through His Word, you will be in His presence. In either of these situations, you cannot enter into His presence without worshipping.

When Abraham was sitting in his tent by the oaks of Mamre, he looked up and saw the Lord (Gen 18:1-15). He immediately did everything necessary to make Him comfortable in his tent. He begged Him to stay and allow him to serve the visitors, he brought water and washed the Lord's feet, commissioned Sarah to make food, and had his servants prepare a calf for his guests. Abraham's actions were actions of worship. He did not simply ask the Lord for information or blessings. Instead, his objective was to see how he could be a servant to the Lord. And he did not do it casually. He *hurried* to tell Sarah to prepare bread, and he asked her to make it *quickly* (v. 6). Then he *ran* to his herd and took one of his *choice* calves and gave it to his servant, who *hurried* to prepare it (v. 7).

Abraham made an extraordinary effort to keep the Lord in his tent. He wanted to stay in His presence and the way he accomplished this was by making the Lord comfortable and by giving Him his best effort. In return, the Lord shared His thoughts with Abraham (v. 17). This conversation, however, was two-sided. After Abraham heard the Lord's plans for Sodom, he engaged Him on the subject of how the city would be disciplined. He was able to ask questions and implore the Lord to change His mind about what He had already decided to do. Abraham bargained with God. God allowed the conversation to continue until He was done. Verse 33 explains that when the Lord had finished speaking to Abraham, He departed and Abraham returned to his place. In other words, the interchange ended when God decided to end it. The same thing happened in 17:22; when God finished explaining to Abraham His instructions to change his and Sarai's names and promising that the two of them will bear a son, He ended the conversation and left.

In many ways, Bible study will mimic this interchange between Abraham and the Lord. Putting aside the impact of modern technology, such as cell phones and email, whenever you speak with someone, you are in their presence. Talking with God is the same way. When you approach Him, or He approaches you, you will find yourself in His presence. When that happens, you must be sure to treat Him with respect and awe, the way Abraham did. Abraham made God comfortable. How can we do the same? By removing anything that would come between us. Obviously, this will mean confessing our sin. We will see this happen in another Scriptural example later. Abraham also worked earnestly to keep God there. He requested Him to stay so that Abraham could provide a service (vs. 3, 4) and he worked urgently to provide that service. Abraham did not serve God lazily or haphazardly. He offered the Lord the best food he had and ensured it was properly prepared. We must be careful to make sure the Lord understands that we are as serious about spending time in His presence as Abraham was.

How would we accomplish such a task? Certainly, God is not going to come and ring our doorbell. We'll never have an opportunity to make Him dinner and have Him relax in the recliner beneath a central air conditioner vent. Abraham was able to make Him physically comfortable. We can't do that so we have to make Him spiritually comfortable. Begin by confessing all your sins. Don't leave anything out. Come clean before Him. Tell Him everything. How many conversations have you tried to have with someone you love and they refused to talk with you because they felt you were hiding something. There was some truth you refused to share and somehow they knew it. They might say to you "since you can't tell me the truth, I have nothing to say to you. Come back and talk to me when you decide to tell me everything that's going on". In the same way, share everything with the Lord. Don't let there be any hindrance to your conversation with Him. Don't force Him to hold back with you just because you're holding back with Him.

Also, remove all distractions when it is time to study. This includes keeping new distractions from appearing during your study time. Make sure your study area is undisturbed. Most of us study at home. If there are children in the house, this can be a real challenge. Even spouses can challenge your effort to eliminate distractions. So how can this be done? First, set a time each day for your study. Your family will probably get used to you being unavailable during that time. I was listening to a pastor explaining how someone wanted to make a large contribution to his church, but to receive it, the pastor would need to meet with the donor at 10 a.m. the next day. The pastor told him he would be unavailable at that time because that was his daily appointment time with God. He was unwilling to allow a donation to distract him from his appointment with God. I usually study late at night after the house has gone quiet. I had gotten used to my wife being an early riser and doing her devotions. I was always a night owl, so I would do my studies late at night after the kids were in bed. I got used to it and even though the kids are now teenagers and I wake earlier than my wife, I still prefer to study at night, even though my teenagers (one in particular) are not usually quiet at night. Also, I prefer there to be no time limit to my study. I don't want to feel rushed because it's time to get to work. When I study at night, I can continue for as long as I need. I'm free to talk with God until He decides it's time to stop, like He did with Abraham.

Next, turn off your electronics. You won't need the television or radio. You might need your phone or computer if you are using web-based tools to facilitate your study, but you can learn to use those tools sparingly so that they don't distract you.

Finally, make a way to handle distractions when they arise. Despite our best efforts, things are bound to happen. With me, they are usually mental. There is always something I need to do that pops into my mind and distracts me. I've learned to just write those things down quickly and push the list aside so I can pay attention to it later.

Just consider, when it's time to have a serious or intimate conversation with someone you need to talk to, whether it's a spouse, work associate, or even a counselor, what do you do? You remove any distractions and guard your time from possible interruptions. You close the office door, or you and your spouse will go to dinner alone, or even take a trip together. You make a serious effort to make your time together intimate. How much more effort should you give to the God who created the universe and everything in it?

After Abraham performed his service, the Lord spoke to him and shared His plans. Abraham was then able to engage the Lord in conversation about those plans. In the same way, when we study Scripture while giving the same type of effort Abraham did, the Lord will, through the Holy Spirit, share insights with us from what we are studying. We can respond to what He is sharing through prayer. We can praise, ask questions, or be sorrowful or repentant. We can converse with the Lord through the Spirit as we study.

Isaiah's worship experience (Isaiah 6:1-13) was similar to Abraham's. He found himself in God's throne room during the year that King Uzziah had died. When he was confronted with the majestic awesomeness of God's presence, he immediately recognized his own unworthiness. He admitted his uncleanness and received a solution from one of the seraphim. A burning coal was taken from the altar and used to clean Isaiah's iniquity. The seraphim states that his iniquity has been removed and his sin had been forgiven (v. 7).

Isaiah's response to God's holiness was classic. I know that sometimes all of us have trouble with humility. We can sometimes think that we can approach God casually and flippantly ask for forgiveness of our sins (because isn't that what we're supposed to do?), get off our knees and go about our business. But Isaiah was seriously distressed about his sinful condition. Once he realized how far short of God's holiness he fell, his solution was to cry out for help.

Here's a recommendation: when you have trouble seeing your sin and your condition the way God sees it, and you find yourself approaching him in prayer or study without seriously confessing your sin, humble yourself in His presence. Do you have trouble with that? Do you find it difficult to humble yourself before God? I know the right answer is to say absolutely not! I know how great God is and I know of His magnificent glory! I understand just how much I fall short of His standard! But speaking practically, do we really? It was easy for Isaiah because he found himself in a position where he was literally seeing God. So what can we do to help us approach God more humbly?

We should take a page out of Job's life and follow his example. Job was afflicted by God for, as far as he knew, no good reason. Job began this ordeal by handling it admirably. Even after his wife advised him to curse God and die because of his calamity (Job 2:9), Job refused to blame God for his condition. But after some time, he became tired of it and he began to justify himself before God as if God had no valid reason for allowing Job to suffer. In Job 31, he exalts himself by explaining how in all social, relational, business, and religious areas, he has always acted righteously. He exclaims that he does not do wrong to anybody, no matter the situation.

Then, in verses 35-40, Job asks for a meeting with God so that he could justify himself. He wanted to prove to God that he did not deserve the punishment he was receiving. God's response to Job begins in chapter 38. Throughout chapters 38 -41, God explains to Job all the things He does and asks Job to prove that he is as good as God by either doing the same things or explaining how they are done. He challenges Job by asking him to gird up his loins like a man (38:3; 40:7), or to ask him if he understands what he has just been told (38:4, 18). In other words, God is comparing Himself to Job and challenging Job to respond. God exclaims that if Job could do what He does, then God will admit that Job is good enough to save himself (40:14).

Job's response was predictable and wise. He proclaims his own folly, repents, and retracts all that he said when he accused God of being unjust.

So what is the lesson we should learn from Job's life about humility? Whenever we have trouble humbling ourselves before God, compare ourselves to Him and the problem is solved. In fact, when I get into the flippant mode, I will sometimes open this passage and read through God's conversation with Job so that I can remind myself of how great He is and of all the great and unexplainable things He does. Then I think about how insignificant I am and humility comes naturally.

So when it is time to enter God's presence for study and we have trouble being serious about confessing our sin and approaching Him with the proper attitude, we can humble ourselves by reminding ourselves of how great He is.

After Isaiah was cleansed, the Lord spoke to him. He asked who He should send on a mission for Us, the Trinity. Isaiah responded by volunteering to perform the service and God gives him specific instruction. Isaiah needs a little clarification, so in verse 11 he asks the Lord "how long?". The Lord answers with more specific information. The experience Isaiah had was similar to the experience Abraham had. Both men found themselves in the Presence of the Lord, and both worshipped. Abraham made an offering to the Lord by preparing food and rest for Him and Isaiah confessed his sin after realizing how unclean he was. The Lord responded to both by allowing each to remain in His presence and sharing with them what He was planning to do or needed someone to do for Him. Both men were allowed to converse with God about His plan.

Bible study has the same elements as these two experiences. When going into God's Word, you want to hear from Him. It is a time for you to seek His instruction, insight, conviction, etc. It is also a time for you to question Him about things you don't understand. Ask Him about circumstances, or about how to apply what He is sharing from the passage you are studying. Just as Abraham and Isaiah needed more specifics, you might need more information. When you do, talk to God about it. If there is something you don't understand, ask for clarification. If there is something He wants from you, but you don't believe you can do it, tell him of your insufficiency and ask Him for help. Moses had to do that when God told him to go to Egypt. He needed help to speak convincingly to Pharaoh, so God sent Aaron to be his mouthpiece.

The lesson here is that when you go to the Word for study, you are going into the presence of God. Act like it. Allow Him to cleanse you by confessing your sin and asking for forgiveness. Make the same effort in your study that Abraham made. Try as hard to understand the Scripture you are studying as Abraham did to make the Lord comfortable in his tent. Let Him speak to you during your study, and don't be afraid to talk to Him and ask questions about what He says. You are bound to get insights about things that are hard for you to understand. You might even be told some things that you might not even agree with, or told to do something you don't want to do (like Moses being told to go to Egypt, or Jonah being commanded to go to Nineveh). If so, be honest with the Lord, like Moses did. Don't try to play like you would do anything for Him when you know (and He knows) you won't. Be honest in your conversation with Him. Moses didn't want to go to Egypt, and he said so. Abraham did not like God's plan for Sodom, and he said so. It's true that Moses ended up going anyway, and God turned out to be right about Sodom. Even Jonah, who disagreed with God about going to Nineveh, ended up going anyway. So don't think that God will always come around to your way of thinking. But it is better for you to confess your doubts and allow Him to instruct you or help (or in Jonah's case, force) you to complete His plans for you.

Give God your earnest effort. Study Scripture as hard as you would study your math book. Do you think Abraham treated the Lord less than he would treat an honored guest in his home? Then in the same way, you should not put more effort into understanding math, or grammar, or aerospace engineering, than you do in knowing God.

If you stand outside in the sun, you will change. You will sweat and your skin will grow darker. You don't even have to do anything, just put yourself in the sun's presence and it will affect you. You won't always notice it immediately, but if you keep exposing yourself to the sun, you will eventually see your skin become tanned. Being in God's presence is like that. You will notice changes in yourself. Not always immediately, but when you compare yourself to how you were back when you began taking Bible study seriously, you will see a difference. You cannot continually place yourself in God's presence and be unchanged.

Bible study is worship. Act like it, and you will see yourself grow closer in relationship to God because you will converse with Him more and more, and as we know, communication is a key to building relationship. God will change you and you will be able to change those around you as you and Him grow closer to each other.

3: Prerequisites to Bible Study

Bible study cannot be accomplished haphazardly. There is a process that must be followed. In fact, the process we are about to discuss is one of many that students can use. Certainly, this process is not the only way to study the Bible, and I usually recommend to students that they learn as many methods as they can. One method might work well for you while another may not help at all.

Generally, there are two types of study: personal and academic. Study that is designed to grow the relationship between you and the Lord is a personal study. Many will use this type of study to replace a daily devotional. They trade the devotional materials they find in bookstores with the process we are about to learn. Instead of reading through material that is designed to be inspirational, they decide to choose a book of Scripture that they want to study and spend time in it daily.

An academic study is done primarily for information. Those who are writing a book report or preparing a sermon or presentation of some sort will need information. Their study will dig out information to help them make their points. I don't mean to say that academic studies can't help you grow, but their intent is to increase knowledge more than relationship. These studies are very useful when you need information, but when relationship building is your focus, a personal study will serve you better.

In a couple of chapters we will discuss topical studies, which can also be either personal or academic. A topical study will allow the student to develop a view or opinion about any particular subject. For example, when election year arrives it would be a good idea to know how to vote. How do you know God's view or thoughts on some of the political issues? If you are to vote as a Christian, you will need to vote the way God would vote if He were going to the booth in your place. A topical study biblically investigates the issues. When complete, you will have a good understanding of what the Bible says about the chosen topic. Obviously, these types of studies can easily become academic, but for the Christian who is trying to grow in relationship and is devoted to pleasing God, he will want to know how to mimic God's thoughts and actions. A topical study can help achieve this. In the same way an ambassador from the United States understands the thoughts and political positions of his superior, the President, the Christian, who is an ambassador for God's Kingdom, must know the thoughts and position God will take on any subject that arises. Topical studies help the Christian achieve this level of knowledge.

However, before we can learn topical studies, we will need to understand Bible studies. The reason for this is that the skills developed in studying a book of the Bible will be needed to study a topic. A Bible study is a study of a particular book of Scripture, so obviously before you can begin, you will need to choose a starting point. However, before you decide where to start, it would be a good idea to get a good study Bible.

Before moving on, it is important to understand the difference between inductive and deductive study. A deductive study happens when the studier approaches the study with a set of presuppositions, or conclusions about the subject of his study. He then searches for information to prove his ideals. Inductive study is the opposite of deductive study. An inductive studier approaches the topic with no conclusions; he will instead develop his conclusions by examining the evidence he gleans from his study. This is the way a good detective conducts an investigation. When a crime has been committed, he examines all of the evidence that he finds and uses it to form a conclusion about how the crime was committed and who committed it. On the other hand, a detective will sometimes assume a crime was committed by a certain person and done a certain way. When he investigates, he will, either purposefully or subconsciously, look for evidence that proves his theory. His method is deductive.

This Bible study method will obviously be inductive. Our intent is to hear from God and develop our ideas and opinions from what He tells us. Our views will adapt as we study deeper, but one of the goals of our study is to allow the Lord to tell us what to think about a matter instead of us telling Him what we think.

Step 1: Choose a Good Study Bible

Study Bibles abound in bookstores everywhere. Both Christian and secular stores will sell them, so how do you decide which to choose?

There are certain characteristics that can make one study Bible more useful than the next. The most important feature is the Bible's accuracy. There is a plethora of versions available. Some are translations, and some are paraphrases. Paraphrases are designed to make the Bible easier to read. Generally, they are not good for serious study, but they can still be useful. Some of the reasons paraphrases are made are valid, while others are not. Initially, they were developed to help those who do not know Christ read the Scripture and understand it more easily. Children's Bibles, for example, are paraphrases. Soon, paraphrases were being developed to help adults understand the Scripture more easily too. But many of them are made for invalid reasons. Certain segments of the population are uncomfortable with what the Bible teaches about certain topics, so a paraphrase will be developed to modify Scripture's teachings so that its message is more palatable. The gender-neutral paraphrases are one example of this. They remove the gender specific terms, like "him" or his, and replace them with general words like "them", "we", "us", or "ours". While this might seem acceptable in certain parts of the Bible, it can easily hide the truth of a passage of Scripture because sometimes when the author uses 'him', he is referring to a male, not just any person. If he does this, there is usually a reason. In other words, the author is trying to make a point. Changing 'him' to 'them' can hide his point and affect the meaning of that passage.

For example, in James 1:23-24, James says that anyone who is a hearer of the word and not a doer is like a man who looks at his face in a mirror and walks away without addressing his faults. The word for man in this passage is the Greek word *aner*, and it is the word used to describe a male. It is sometimes used to describe a husband, but it is not ever used to describe a female or a person in general. The word *anthropos* is generally used to describe a person, or a general group of people. Why would James use the word "male" in this passage instead of the word "person"?

Think about the illustration he is using. Consider the difference between a man examining himself in a mirror and a woman examining herself in a mirror. She would be much more likely to find every fault, no matter how tiny it might be, and address it. When she's done, the fault would be eradicated, even if it takes hours. A man is more likely to take a quick glance, splash some water on his face, run his hand over his hair really quick, and leave. He hasn't studied his face in an attempt to detect issues that would compromise his 'beauty'. Also consider that the mirrors in James' day were not the highly reflective surfaces we have today, and the light they used was probably firelight or a lantern of some sort. Examining yourself with a lantern in a mirror that was probably made of polished brass or another metal would be a monumental task, especially for a male. A female is more likely to endure the process and do it thoroughly. A male is more likely to skip as much of the process as he can.

James knew this, so when he describes the relationship a Christian should have to the Word of God, he says that they should relate to the Bible the way a woman would to a mirror, not the way a man would. A woman who uses the mirror to find faults would use the same mirror to fix those faults. Once she worked her magic, the mirror would tell her if she did a good job. Scripture is like this. It will not only show you your sin, but it will let you know if you did a good job of addressing it. This is the point James is trying to make. If he had used the word *anthropos*, there is a good chance his meaning would have gone undetected.

A translation is designed to be as close as possible to the original Hebrew, Aramaic, and Greek manuscripts. A translation is made from the manuscripts, while a paraphrase is generally made from a translation.

The New American Standard (NASB) translation was developed to be grammatically correct and true to the original manuscripts. Because this was the goal of the Lockman Foundation, the group that is responsible for the NASB, it is considered to be the most accurate translation available. One reason for this is that the NASB was translated directly from the original manuscripts, while several (not all) other Bibles were translated from previous translations, not the original manuscripts. Some were actually designed to be improvements to an earlier translation.

As accurate as translations try to be, there are times when they will change the text of Scripture in order to make it easier to read in modern language. For example, some translations will remove the "Thee's" and "Thou's" of Scripture and replace them with "You" and "Yours". It makes it easier to digest without changing the meaning of the text.

Another feature found in some study bibles is the use of italics to indicate words that were not found in the original languages, but are implied by it. The words *referring* and *rather* in Galatians 3:16 are examples of this. Adding these terms does not change the meaning of the Scripture, but makes it easier to read and understand in English. Sometimes also, the translation will detect the need to change the grammar of a passage in order to properly translate the manuscript in certain passages. In the introductory material found at the beginning of these bibles, that process will be adequately defined. The publisher will explain what was done and the reasons for doing it. How to detect the changes will also be explained in the introductory material.

There are several characteristics of study bibles that make them useful. First, a good study bible will be an accurate translation. We spoke a little about that in the above section. There are clues to a book author's message that can sometimes be missed when reading an inaccurate version of Scripture. The use of repetitive words for example, is a good way to see a main point an author is trying to make. We'll talk more about repetition in a later section, but many bibles that are specialized will change some of these words. When they do, certain clues to the meaning of some passages are hidden. This can make it difficult to see some of the teachings the author is trying to relay. An accurate translation will allow the student to see as closely as possible what the writer put on paper, which will help understand more clearly the message he is trying to portray.

Next, each book of a study bible will have an introduction. This is a section that gives some background information about the book. It can kick start your study by providing insight into the author's intent and into the situation he might have been writing about. Even though introductions are included in almost all study Bibles, you will inevitably use extra-biblical sources to get much of your introductory information.

You should also look for wide margins in a study bible. These will give you room to make notes. The paper quality is also important. Study bibles get marked up quite a bit. Many students like using highlighters or colored pencils to mark passages. A more durable page can take more marking and handling.

Other tools that are usually found in these bibles are concordances, maps, timelines, and cross references. Some will also have Hebrew and Greek lexicons so the student can examine the meaning of some key words in their original languages. More extensive versions of each of these tools can be found as reference materials in Christian bookstores everywhere, and they will sometimes be needed in order to understand some of Scripture's clues.

Another good and very important quality of a study bible is the marking of paragraphs. Serious study requires the student to know where a paragraph begins and ends. Different publishers will mark these different ways. The most common method is to bold the number of the verse that begins a paragraph. More will be said about this later. Sometimes, bibles are written in paragraph form already, like a normal book, and each paragraph is clearly separated from the ones surrounding it. For example, bibles that are thin to save space and make the Bible easier to carry are usually written like this.

It is very important to read the instructions of whichever study bible you choose. All the tools it contains will only be useful if you know how to use them. The introductions of these bibles explain the tools that they contain so that you can make the best use of them. As you develop your study skills, you might find that you need the tools a study bible provides less frequently that you did at first, but it is always good to have access to them in case they are needed.

Step 2: Gather the Needed Study Tools

After making your list, use some of the study tools listed below to begin searching for information. Of course, you will not need all the reference material listed here for every passage you study.

Exhaustive Concordance	This book is an index of every word found in the Bible. They are made for each translation, since each translation uses different words. For example, the King James Version has an exhaustive concordance that cannot be used for a New American Standard Bible. This book also translates the words into their original language.
Expository Dictionary	This book will give a detailed analysis of a word in its original language. After finding the word in the concordance, you would use this book to determine its meaning.
Topical Bible	This is a book that lists a variety of topics in alphabetical order. Under each topic will be a list of scriptures in their entirety that refer to that topic. This book is not exhaustive because it does not list all the verses in the Bible that pertain to a particular topic. Examples of topics that are found are prayer, forgiveness, and anger.
Bible Dictionary	This book will provide details about some of the background items in Scripture. For example, you would find information on Jerusalem. Bethlehem, the Pharisees, Nazarite vows, etc.

Bible Introduction	Many study Bibles have an introduction at the beginning of every book. The Bible introduction is similar, but more detailed. For example, you would find information regarding the author, the intended audience, the date of writing, the subject of the writing and the historical milieu.
Commentary	This book will explain each verse of Scripture. There are numerous commentaries and are useful for introductions and outlines of each book. Be careful to use them only as a tool and not as a crutch.
Bible Encyclopedias	This book will give insight into the general culture of the time the book you are studying was written. It will give information such as weights and measures, types of currency, types of work, and family life.
Bible Atlas	An atlas of the biblical territories can help you understand the geographical relationship between nations. It can shed light on how geography can either hinder or promote certain actions or relationships between regions.

In addition to the reference materials listed above, many students will use online resources for their study. Most have access to the internet away from home on mobile devices and these websites are usually free. Some will also allow you to save your study notes so you can pick up where you left off the next time you enter the website. You can write on these sites just like you were keeping a notebook at home. This allows more flexibility for the student and the savings from not having to buy reference materials can be tremendous.

Step 3: Choose a Starting Point

The Bible is usually studied one testament at a time. This is a logical way to progress and it would make it easier to assimilate our information so we can better understand the truth of God's Word. Usually, the New Testament is a good place to begin, so for our lesson, we will use the New Testament as an example.

However, there is no rule that says you need to study the Bible in any particular order. There are many factors that may influence your decision about where to begin. If, for example, you are curious about certain facets of Old Testament history or culture, you may want to study the Old Testament first.

After choosing a testament, we need to decide which section to study first (see the table below). Again, there are many factors that can influence your choice. These sections do not need to be studied in order, even though that is the way the New Testament is usually done. Neither do all the books in a section need to be studied consecutively, even though that could make your study easier.

Sections of the Bible (Authors in parentheses)

OLD TESTAMENT	NEW TESTAMENT
The Pentateuch	The Gospels
Genesis (Moses)	Matthew (Matthew)
Exodus (Moses)	Mark (Mark)
Leviticus (Moses)	Luke (Luke)
Numbers (Moses)	John (John)
Deuteronomy (Moses)	
	History
Pre-exilic History	Acts (Luke)
Joshua (Joshua)	
Judges (Unknown)	Pauline Epistles
Ruth (Unknown)	Epistles to the Churches
1 & 2 Samuel (Unknown)	Romans (Paul)
1 & 2 Kings (Unknown)	1 & 2 Corinthians (Paul)
	Galatians (Paul)
Post-exilic History	Ephesians (Paul)
1 & 2 Chronicles (Unknown, possibly Ezra)	Philippians (Paul)
Ezra (Ezra)	Colossians (Paul)
Nehemiah (Nehemiah)	1 & 2 Thessalonians (Paul)
Esther (Unknown)	
	Pastoral Epistles
Poetical Books	1 & 2 Timothy (Paul)
Job (Unknown)	Titus (Paul)
Psalms (David and others)	Philemon (Paul)
Proverbs (Solomon and others)	

Ecclesiastes (Solomon)	
Song of Solomon (Solomon)	General Epistles
	Hebrews (Unknown, possibly Barnabas)
Major Prophets	James (James)
Isaiah (Isaiah)	1 & 2 Peter (Peter)
Jeremiah (Jeremiah)	1, 2, 3 John (John)
Lamentations (Jeremiah)	Jude (Jude)
Ezekiel (Ezekiel)	
Daniel (Daniel)	Apocalyptic (Prophecy)
	Revelation (John)
Minor Prophets	
Hosea (Hosea)	
Joel (Joel)	
Amos (Amos)	
Obadiah (Obadiah)	
Jonah (Jonah)	
Micah (Micah)	
Nahum (Nahum)	
Habakkuk (Habakkuk)	
Zephaniah (Zephaniah)	
Haggai (Haggai)	
Zechariah (Zechariah)	
Malachi (Malachi)	

The first book in the section is usually the best place to begin. But sometimes the first book in a section is too difficult of a place to start. When this is the case, it is a good idea to find another book in the same section to begin studying. After becoming comfortable with lesser material, you can attack the more difficult book. Sometimes all the writings of a particular author are studied, even if they cross into other sections. John's writings, for example, are found in the Gospels, the General Epistles, and the Apocalyptic sections. Taking this route can help your study because you might notice certain characteristics of a particular writer's style or vocabulary that he uses throughout his writings. Understanding some of these can help you when you are studying his writings.

Step 4: Complete a Book Introduction

Before beginning your study, complete an introduction to the book you have chosen. The objective is to acquire a good general understanding of the content. An introduction will give as much ancillary information as possible about the book. It will usually begin by revealing the author and the prospective audience and continues by determining the reason for the writing. The historical or societal background that surrounds our book might also be discussed because it could shed more light on the book's meaning. Understanding the times in which the book was written can help you understand what is happening.

An introduction will also attempt to analyze the state of the author or culture at the time of the book's writing to shed light on its meaning. For example, the introduction may tell of any personal feelings the author may have had when he wrote the book. Or it may tell about the relationship of Israel to the nation from where the book is written. It may even give an idea of what the readers were experiencing or the author's relationship to them. This will provide insight into the reason for its writing.

Introductions are primarily academic, and to find the necessary information, you will need to consult several outside sources. These sources can include Bible dictionaries, Bible surveys, Bible handbooks, and Bible encyclopedias. In addition, almost all study bibles have introductions preceding each book, which are usually short and informative. Some of the cursory details about the book can often be found there. The author will be named and his intent for writing the book along with any available background information will usually be explained.

Commentaries can be used, but only for the introduction. They are not a good resource to use once you begin studying the text. A commentary will explain the meaning of each verse of a biblical book. If you are trying to build a relationship with the Lord, you really do not want others telling you what a passage means; you want to find out for yourself. It's just like getting to know someone you are interested in. You probably don't want to learn about them from what someone else says. You want to get to know them for yourself. You would approach them and strike up a conversation and over time a relationship might develop. For this reason, book introductions found in commentaries can be a good source of background information that you can use to grow your understanding of its content. Beyond that, commentaries should be ignored for a personal study. If, however, your study is academic, a good commentary can be a valuable resource.

There are also resources called, oddly enough, introductions. These will usually reference either the Old or New Testaments, although some will cover the entire Bible. The information found in these books is extensive. They can reveal historical issues related to politics and culture. They can also be informative about religions, their rites, and their impact. Sometimes, having this type of information can help the student better understand the writer, the readers, and the circumstances around the book's writing.

Bible atlases can also be helpful. Sometimes, geographical details can shed light on who is involved and why they might be involved. It can help you understand some circumstances and how or why they could impact what might be happening.

Another source of introductory material is Scripture itself. Some books of the Bible can be better understood by studying parts of other books. This is especially true when reading through the Old Testament prophets. For example, Isaiah 1:1 says that he was active during the reigns of Uzziah, Jotham, Ahaz, and Hezekiah. Before studying this book, it would probably be helpful to read 2 Kings 18 – 21. That is the passage that describes some details about what was happening while Isaiah was prophesying. It will be easier to understand Isaiah's thoughts when you know what was happening in Israel during his life.

When Paul writes Colossians, he is combatting a heresy known as Gnosticism. The Gnostics believed that matter and thought were separate. Matter was evil, and thought was the source of salvation. Material was evil, and this is why they refused to attribute a physical body to Christ. To them, His body only appeared real, but it was obviously just an apparition. This belief developed into two factions. The first faction believed that since the body was evil, it should be made to suffer. For this reason, they reveled in self-discipline and the harsh treatment of the body. They would abstain from certain activities that gave the body pleasure, such as the consumption of certain foods.

The other faction believed that since the body was evil, it did not make any sense to restrain it. After all, evil bodies do what evil bodies do, right? Consequently, this faction allowed the body to completely indulge itself. They engaged in all sorts of sexual and sensory pleasures that the other faction tried to avoid.

Knowing these facts gives the student a clearer picture of the content. When doing the overview, which is the next step in our process, certain details which might have gone unnoticed, will be seen and will help clarify Colossians' message. This is the main reason for putting together a book introduction.

The tools that are used for book introductions can be found in libraries or in bookstores. They can be very expensive, especially if you want to own a complete set. Going to and from the library can be inconvenient. A better choice is to find these resources online. There are several good Bible study sites that allow you to document your work and save it so you can build on it. We spoke a little about these types of sites earlier. They are usually free, and they contain all of the study tools you will need to do your work. Using them can save time and expense.

After meeting these prerequisites, you can proceed to your study. Understand that doing well at each step of this process makes the succeeding step easier. For example, finding a good study Bible makes your introduction easier. Also, finding good resources will make your introduction more thorough. When you build your introduction, keep in mind that the better and more complete your introduction, the easier your study of the book that you chose will be. Now, let's move to the next step of the process.

4: STUDY THE BOOK

After the preliminary work of gathering the necessary tools and completing a book introduction, it is time to begin studying the book you have chosen a little at a time until you have studied the entire book. Oddly enough, the first step in studying the book piece by piece is to study it as a whole. This is accomplished by doing an overview of your chosen book.

Step 1: Overview the Book

The first thing you must do when overviewing a book is read it thoroughly several times. This will give you an understanding of the book's general topic. Even if the book addresses several topics (e.g.,1 Corinthians), you will need to know that. If you have done your introduction properly, you will have a head start because you will already have a general understanding of the issues that necessitated the book's writing. Remember, Bible study, like building a relationship, cannot always be rushed. You will gather a lot of information while completing an overview of the book you've chosen, but the information is not the goal. Take all the time you need to hear from the Lord about what you are seeing. Write down your observations so you can build on them and refer to them later. When questions arise, take time to pray and meditate on what you notice. Sometimes, an overview can take months, especially with the larger or more difficult books. This is not a rush job. Focus on the process, not the information that will be gleaned from following the process. Some will have more time than others to devote to daily study. This will, of course, affect how quickly or slowly you progress through your study.

Observation is a key tactic when completing your overview. Pay attention to every fact you notice, even the tiniest ones. They might not make sense immediately, but the more you go through the book and more observations you make, they will begin to fit together.

Observation is a tool that you will use at almost every step of your study. As you build your study skills, your ability to observe will develop naturally. Some of the tools you will use to gather data from the Scriptures will force you to either notice or find things in the passage you're studying. After a while, it will become habitual. You will cease to force yourself to make observations in the passages you study. In fact, you might not be able to stop making them.

Your observations will produce questions. This is normal and desired. Your questions will create conversations with the Lord. When you are reading His Book and there is something you do not understand, He is the best person to talk to about it. We will continue to discuss this characteristic of making observations as we move forward.

When reading, do it **thoughtfully** and **prayerfully**. Read as if you were having a conversation with the Author. When He says something you do not understand, ask Him what He means. As you think and meditate on what you're reading, pray that you will understand the meaning. Developing a relationship with the Lord is a lot like developing a relationship with anyone. You get to know each other by communicating. As you talk, questions are sure to come up. When they do, you would usually ask them and expect answers. This would probably generate more questions, which you would ask and then wait for answers. This process of communicating with others is basic to forming and building relationships. The more you and your counterpart talk, the better you will get to know each other.

The entire process of Bible study centers around listening to and talking to God, but unlike talking to our friends face to face, He talks to us through His Word, the Bible, and we talk to Him through prayer. Studying Scripture is how we listen to what He wants to say to us, and prayer is how we respond to Him or ask Him questions about what He says.

Generating questions is one of the best ways to grow closer to the Lord. The more questions that arise about what you are reading, the more you will need to go to Him for the answers. This process creates more consistent, more intense communication. This is what you desire, because one thing that characterizes deeper relationships is deeper communication. Hearing the Lord will not always result in questions, however. Sometimes it will force a response of praise, sorrow, or reflection that you will need to address with Him. This can also intensify your communication and your relationship with Him.

A good way to generate questions about what you're reading is to use your **imagination** on the passages. Imagine the situations or circumstances the people were experiencing and think about their difficulties, or victories. Put yourself in their situation and see if you can imagine how they might feel, or what they might think. Many of us have done this from time to time anyway. For example, how many times have you mentally chastised the Israelites because they always seem to walk away from God? Don't you usually say something like "if I was living back then, and God spoke from heaven (like He did back then), I would never walk away. How could I when I see all the awesome stuff He does all the time? My allegiance would be strong. I wouldn't forsake Him just because things got a little tough. Those Israelites were crybabies. They didn't know how good they have it compared to what we have today. I would know exactly what He wanted from me and I would do it! I'd always remember how He parted the Red Sea and I would give Him my everlasting love! I don't understand what was wrong with those people back then – always leaving God, getting in trouble, and then come crawling back! Man, how selfish can you get?" But what we fail to understand is that many of these events took place years apart. Your grandparents may have heard God speak from Heaven, but maybe you haven't. The Red Sea might have been parted in front of your great grandparents, but when have you ever seen a miracle?

Also keep in mind that there wasn't a church on every corner in Israel. There weren't preachers in every neighborhood. The nation usually only had one or two prophets, and if you wanted to see one, you either had to travel to his city or wait for him to decide to travel to yours. In addition, Israel was prime territory for business travel. Business caravans would cross Israel from east to west to do business.

Well, these business people did not worship the Jewish God, they had their own god to worship. To honor their gods during travel, they would erect temples of some sort so they could pay homage to their god as they traveled. These caravans were most likely the source of the Asherah poles found throughout Israel. The Israelites might not have originally erected these poles, but they certainly fell into the worship of the god or goddess these shrines were designed to honor. It is possible that some Israelites saw more worship of Baal and Asherah in their lives than they saw worship of God. Under these circumstances, it is a little easier to understand how difficult it might have been to keep an allegiance to God and how easy it must have been to worship gods that might have seemed more real.

So the Israelites didn't have it as easy as most of us think. Once you realize how difficult it was for them to stay true to God, maybe you'll change your mind about how firmly you would stand when things got tough.

Think about this scenario and use your imagination. In Matthew 2:16 Herod orders all the male children who are two years old and under that live in the Bethlehem area to be slain. Suppose you were one of the soldiers commissioned to carry out this order, but you had a nephew who lived in Bethlehem that was two years old? How would you feel about Herod's order? What would you do? What would the consequences be for doing the wrong thing? What are the consequences for doing the right thing? Do you even know what the right thing to do is? Could you do something you might not want to do no matter how you felt about it? After meditating and praying about this, think about a situation like this that might have arisen in your life (not life threatening, of course). What if no matter which decision you made, there would be consequences. What would you do? Or if it was a situation from your past, what did you do? Using your imagination to try feeling like they might have felt can be a good way to search yourself and deal with this type of situation if it arises one day, or to revisit it if it has happened in the past.

Not all questions need to be generated. There are a few questions you should commonly ask yourself while overviewing your book. Those questions are: who, what, why, when, and where? These questions can be useful in helping you understand more about what you are reading. They can help you dig out hidden facts and allow you to carefully consider how they might shed some light on the passage you are reading. The answers to these questions will be more useful in some passages than they are in others, but it is a good idea to get into the habit of asking them in each passage you study.

In 1 Kings 18: 16 – 46, Elijah is having a feud with the prophets of Baal and Asherah. Examine this passage and consider who is involved in this story. Who are the active participants? Who are the spectators? Who is the real cause of all this commotion? Is it Elijah, King Ahab, or the prophets of Baal and Asherah. Could the people actually be the real cause of the trouble?

What is going on in this passage? What are the Prophets of Baal doing? What is Elijah doing? What is King Ahab doing? What was he doing while Elijah was slaying the prophets of Baal (without his permission)? What do you think King Ahab was going to tell his wife Jezebel about what happened? What does Elijah hope to accomplish by doing this? What effect should it have on the people of Israel? What effect did it have?

Where was King Ahab while the prophets were being slain? Was he even there? Where is this incident taking place?

Why is this happening? Why is it necessary? Why did the prophets of Baal become so self-destructive in their worship? Was this normal? Why did Elijah taunt them? Why did Elijah ask the people to come near when it was time for him to call on God?

When is this taking place? When did it begin? When did it end?

There won't always be answers to these questions, but that should not keep you from asking them. Many times, as in the above example, the questions can be expanded upon to create more questions. This is a normal process and it can be helpful in digging out more information.

Here's another example. Try this one on your own. See which other questions can be generated from the basic ones then answer them from the passage. Take your time, this is not always a quick process.

Read **Genesis 11:1 – 9**. Record your observations about the following questions.

Who is involved in this account?
_____
_____
_____

What are they doing?
_____
_____
_____

Why are they doing it?
_____
_____
_____

When is this taking place?
_____
_____
_____

Where is it taking place?
_____
_____
_____

How did you do? Did some of these questions lead to more who, what, why, when, and where questions? Remember, questions create conversation with God, and the goal of deeper conversation is deeper relationship.

Reading **meditatively** is another good way to understand the Scripture being studied. Turn the Scripture over and over in your mind until the Holy Spirit sheds light on what you are reading. Work on it the same way you would a math problem that you had trouble understanding. If you worked it and got the wrong answer, you would study it to find your error. Then you would re-work it to get another answer. You would keep at it until you got the correct answer. Sometimes the problem is too tough for you to figure it out on your own. In that case, you would need to get help. There are several sources of help to resolve a math problem. You could ask a tutor, or your math teacher, but what if you had access to the author of the math book? Suppose you could call him and have him walk you through the problem? Wouldn't that be more valuable and more enlightening? Wouldn't you be more confident in your understanding if it came from the author rather than a tutor? Meditating on Scripture can be just as difficult as working a math problem. Sometimes you will need help. Where can you find it? Many assume that the place to go would be to a commentary to read an expert's explanation of the passage. But what if you had access to the Author of Scripture? Wouldn't it be better to gain your understanding from Him? Understanding Scripture from talking to the Lord is better in the same way that learning math from the author is better than learning it from a tutor. This does not mean, by any stretch of the imagination, that we should not go to our pastors, mentors, teachers, or friends and family who might be able to shed light on a difficult passage of Scripture. But we should be very careful about depending too heavily on their explanations of Scripture. Not because they might be wrong, but because you want, as often as possible, to talk with God about what you are seeing in His Word. Remember that your goal is to grow your relationship with Him, not just learn more stuff about Him.

Finally, read **patiently** and **repeatedly**. You won't be able to gather every clue or understand every message the author is trying to relay with only one reading. The more times you read through the book, the better you will understand it because you will notice more details each time. Don't be in a hurry to overview the book. The more thorough your overview, the easier it will be to study the details when you reach the next step of Bible study. In the same way a good introduction makes an overview easier, a good overview makes Bible study easier. Again, overviews can take several weeks of constantly reading the book through and making observations. Sometimes, it can take months. Several factors might affect this. Maybe you are studying one of the larger books, or maybe you don't have much time to spend each day in deep study. Whatever the reason, don't be afraid to take your time with the overview. Building a relationship with the Lord is not always a quick process; in fact, it is rarely a quick process. Take all the time you need. If you are studying for academic reasons, you can move through the book as fast as you want because you can search other resources, like commentaries, to get the information you need to build your knowledge base. But if your desire is relationship, it will take time. Remember, it's not about how much you know; rather, it's about how much you grow.

    When we made a quick introduction of Colossians in the previous section, we discovered that Paul was writing to battle a heresy known as Gnosticism. While preparing an overview, we can detect certain ways Paul is fighting this belief system. Notice how Paul exalts Christ early in the book. During his description of the preeminence of Christ in 1:13-23, Paul slyly mentions that He made peace through the blood of His cross and that He had a fleshly body (vs. 20, 23). Remember the Gnostics believed that Christ did not have a body since flesh was inherently evil. Paul also used the term bodily form (2:9) to describe Christ. He was making it clear that Christ had a physical, earthly body. Paul also mentioned, in contrast to the

Gnostics' belief that wisdom is found in knowledge, that all the treasures of wisdom and knowledge are found in Christ (2:3).

Paul also instructs the Colossian church to fight heresies that can be deceptive (2:4, 8, 16-23). There's no doubt he was warning them to fight off the Gnostic influence that was attacking the church. He draws a line between Christian and Gnostic living beginning in 2:16 by instructing the Colossians to stop letting others rob them of their prize by insisting on strange physical disciplines. He continues in 3:1ff by describing the mindset and behavior of those who belong to Christ. He mentions that we have laid aside the old self and its evil practices (3:9-10) and argues against fleshly indulgence and useless abstinence, both descriptive of the two extremes of Gnosticism (3:1-8 and 2:20-23). These arguments, along with the instruction about our bodies being dead to the same types of sins that some Gnostics freely engage in, are directly aimed at the Gnostic philosophy.

In this book, Paul uses the words flesh or fleshly six times and the words body or bodily ten times. Clearly, he is making a contrast between the beliefs of the Gnostics and the Christians. Without completing a good introduction, most of these facts would have gone unnoticed. Hopefully, while doing your overview, you would have noticed the consistent repetition of the words mentioned above, but without understanding the reason for the letter, you would be missing much of the detail that could enhance your understanding of the point Paul is trying to make. So you can see how a solid introduction can enhance your overview.

Again, relationships take time. If you were building a relationship with a person, you would expect to have long and intimate conversations with that person. The more time you spent with them, the more questions you would have. Asking those questions would lead to a deeper level of intimacy between the two of you because the conversation would grow increasingly intense. If a relationship with a human takes much time and effort, how much more would a relationship with the God of the universe take? After all, if you are willing to make the effort to get to know someone, how much more effort should you be willing to expend to get to know God?

Overviews are essential to your study and they will take a lot of time. The longer you spend on your overview, the closer you will grow to the Lord and the easier your study will be when you begin digging into the details of the book.

When you were young and your sweetie sent you a love letter, you read it time after time and poured over every detail. You wondered what she meant when she said you were cool. What did she mean by that? How was she feeling when she wrote it? You would analyze that letter until you understood it completely. Then you would read it again and analyze it one more time. Studying the Scripture is much like reading a love letter. You analyze it and wonder about it and read it all over again. Once you understand it, or you think you understand it, you start all over.

Reading over that letter time after time created questions that you did not know how to answer. Overviewing the Bible has the same tendency. You will generate questions that you cannot answer, and just like getting the answer to your questions about the love letter is best accomplished by approaching its author, getting answers to your questions about Scripture is best accomplished by approaching its Author. Those questions produce conversation, and conversation is a building block of relationship, which is the goal of Bible study.

Your overview will lead to the discovery of the book's parts, or sections. As you read the book repeatedly, you will begin noticing changes of focus or subject at different points in the book. For example, a book's main topic may be about faith. But the first part may explain true faith. The second part may analyze the readers' faith and find it to be deficient. The third part may instruct the readers on how to correct themselves so their faith meets God's standard. These might be the main sections of your book that you notice at first. Further observation might reveal more sections. When you move to the next step of Bible study, you will probably end up fine tuning your divisions. Your closer examination of the text will clarify your overview, which is a more general survey of the book. When you are sure your overview is complete, it will be time to move to the next step.

Step 2: Divide the Book's Parts into Passages

After separating the book into parts, you need to identify the chapters or passages that compose each part. Actually, you have already performed this exercise when you did your book overview. This step is inserted for outlining purposes. It helps you organize the study to make it more beneficial. Here is an example of an outline of all the information you have acquired to this point about the book you are studying.

Introduction to Galatians

Paul wrote Galatians to nullify the false doctrines that had been introduced by the Judaizers. These doctrines perverted Christianity into a type of legalism. The Judaizers were able to convince the Galatians to abandon Paul's teachings and defect to theirs.

There were two reasons the Judaizers were able to accomplish this. First, the Galatians were easily convinced to change their minds, they were too impressionable. Second, the Judaizers were able to cast doubt on Paul's authority by challenging his apostleship.

I   Greeting 1:1-5

II   Chastisement of Galatians 1:6-10

III   Defense of Paul's Apostleship 1:11-2:21
    A Origin of his apostleship 1:11-24
    B Development of his apostleship 2:1-10
    C Test of his apostleship

IV   Refuting the Judaizers 3:1-3:29
    A Christians are free from the Law 3:1-14
    B The intent of the Law 3:15-29

V   Adoption into God's Family 4:1-31
    A We are sons, not slaves 4:1-20
    B We are free from the Law 4:21-31

> VI How Should We Live as Free Men? 5:1-6:10
>   *A* Stand firm, don't go backward 5:1-12
>   *B* Serve each other 5:13-15
>   *C* Walk by the Spirit 5:16-26
>   *D* Help those who are burdened 6:1-5
>   *E* Do good to all men 6:6-10
>
> VII Closing 6:11-18

This example taken from Galatians is by no means exhaustive. There are more subsections to some of the outline points shown here. This example is given as a template to show the kind of divisions you should see after an overview of the book you are studying. As you move forward from the overview into the study of each separate paragraph, your outline will become more detailed and more accurate. You will be able to add clarity because the details you see in the paragraphs will amplify your understanding of the book's content.

For some, a chart works better than an outline. A chart will organize the information found in your overview into a format that shows a quick survey of the skeleton of your book. At this point, there won't be any real details in the chart, just a basic survey of the book's content. During the next step, as you go deeper into your book, you will, if you would like to, be able to clarify and enhance the chart so that it becomes more detailed.

Step 3: Determine the Paragraphs in the Passages

Most of the study bibles and a few others have already marked the paragraphs in the passages of Scripture. Some publishers identify the paragraphs by placing the symbol ¶ in front of the verse that begins a new paragraph. But most publishers identify a new paragraph by **bolding** the verse number of the paragraph's beginning. Here is an example from the book of James chapter one (NASB):

> **1.** James, a bond-servant of God and of the Lord Jesus Christ, to the twelve tribes who are dispersed abroad, greetings.
> **2.** Consider it all joy, my brethren, when you encounter various trials,
> 3. Knowing that the testing of your faith produces endurance.
> 4. And let endurance have its perfect result, that you may be perfect and complete, lacking in nothing.
> **5.** But if any of you lacks wisdom, let him ask of God, who gives to all men generously and without reproach, and it will be given to him.

In this example, the paragraphs begin in verses 1, 2, and 5. Sometimes, paragraphs begin in the middle of a verse. When that happens, the first letter of the first word in the paragraph will be **bolded**. An example can be found in Genesis 37:2. A new paragraph begins with the word "Joseph". Notice that the "J" is **bolded**. Again, each publisher has their own habits of marking paragraphs. Some publishers will mark paragraphs that begin in the middle of a verse, and others will ignore them.

Some bibles are already written in paragraph format. Most paraphrases, such as the Living Bible, that are designed for easy reading are written like this. Reading these bibles are the same as picking up a novel. Other bibles that are specialized can also be written in paragraph format. For example, bibles that have a thinline format are designed to be smaller and easier to carry. They are in paragraph format because much space is saved when every verse is not indented.

After identifying the paragraphs, it is time to study them in detail.

Step 4: Study the Paragraphs

This is where the hard work begins. Paragraphs in Scripture are the fundamental building blocks that are used to form the themes and topics that are so important to understanding God's message. You will find that many of the skills you used while overviewing the book will also be used to study the individual paragraphs.

Every paragraph has a theme. Your goal is to find that theme and compare it to the theme of the preceding paragraph and the theme of the succeeding paragraph. This is essentially accomplished by **meditation and prayer**, but the beginning of your paragraph study will be another exercise in observation. Remember when you overviewed the book? If your overview was complete, you will probably already have a good idea of the general meaning of the paragraph you are about to study. Even if this is true, it is a good idea to spend a few minutes making a new observation of the paragraph.

Joshua 1: 8 instructs us to meditate on God's word. Meditation simply means to take Scripture and turn it over and over in your mind until you understand what it means. The understanding you receive from your exercise comes from the Holy Spirit. His job is to illumine the meaning of Scripture to you.

The Holy Spirit is essential to every believer. His ministry to us allows us to function in a relationship with our Heavenly Father. The functions He performs are generally focused around keeping us in fellowship with God. The ministry of Jesus Christ has reconciled us to the Father, and the ministry of the Spirit keeps us close to Him.

Some of the functions the Spirit performs include regeneration of sinners, conversion, sanctification of believers, indwelling of believers, and guiding. All of these ministries to us are essential to the growth of our relationship to God.

John 14:26 says:

> "But the Helper, the Holy Spirit, whom the Father will send in my name, He will teach you all things, and bring to your remembrance all that I said to you."

And 1 John 2:27 says:

> And as for you, the anointing which you received from Him abides in you, and you have no need for anyone to teach you; but as His anointing teaches you about all things, and is true

and is not a lie, and just as it has taught you, you abide in Him.

These scriptures make it clear that our primary instructor in spiritual matters is the Holy Spirit. He illuminates the words and messages of Scripture to us. The Lord promises that when we need understanding the Holy Spirit will provide it.

1 Corinthians 2:11-13:

> 11 For who among men knows the thoughts of a man except the spirit of the man, which is in him? Even so the thoughts of God no one knows except the Spirit of God.
> 12 Now we have received, not the spirit of the world, but the Spirit who is from God, that we might know the things freely given to us by God,
> 13 which things we also speak, not in words taught by human wisdom, but in those taught by the Spirit, combining spiritual thoughts with spiritual words.

Even though the Lord has provided teachers to help us with our study of Scripture, their role is secondary to the role of the Holy Spirit in helping us understand God's word. They are the messengers we spoke of earlier. Who better to explain the teachings of the Lord than the Lord Himself? We have the Holy Spirit indwelling us and when we need to know what God is trying to say to us, the best thing to do is ask Him to explain, and according to the above passages, He will.

Let's revisit the math example we used earlier. When you used to do your math homework there would always be a problem that would be a little difficult. You would work it out the best you could, then look in the back of the book for the answer, only to find that your answer was wrong. You would then redo the problem to find your mistake. You'd check again to see if your answer was correct. If not, you would redo it again and again until you found where you were making your mistake, then you would move to the next problem.

Meditating on Scripture is just like meditating on math. You continue to work on it until you get it right.

There are additional methods you can use in the study of paragraphs. Commentaries are a good source of information on difficult passages. But these should only be used in an academic study. You should always attempt to get every bit of information without any help outside of the Holy Spirit.

Sometimes the author will leave clues in a paragraph or group of paragraphs that, if you can find them, will help you see the important points he is trying to make. Some of these clues will sometimes exist in certain paragraphs, and other times they will be noticed either throughout the book or across several paragraphs. Obviously, when these clues occur throughout the entire book, they will be more easily noticed during the overview stage of your study. But even if you miss them, you can catch them while completing a detailed study of the book's passages.

One of these clues is **repetition**. Look for words or terms that are repeated. When you see them, it may mean the author is trying to draw your attention to them. In John 15: 4-11 is a single paragraph. In that paragraph, you can see the word *abide* repeated 11 times.

Obviously, John is trying to emphasize the importance of staying connected to our Savior.

1 Corinthians 12 is another good example of repetition. This is an example of repetition spread across several paragraphs. Read through that chapter and notice how many times you see the word *body*. Read it again and notice the word *members*. Read it again and notice the word *Spirit*. Read it again and notice the word *all*. What message must Paul be trying to send to his audience about the Church? If you completed your overview of 1 Corinthians, you would know that one of the problems this church was experiencing was a lack of unity. They had developed factions, and these factions were aligning themselves with different preachers (1Cor. 1:10-13). Paul uses the physical body as an illustration of what the church body should be. This is his way of explaining how unity in the Church should look. Repetition of the words listed above draw the readers' attention to the emphasis he is placing on the body and how its members are tied to and unified with each other.

Try this exercise:

> Examine **Titus 2 -3**. Look for words or phrases that are repeated and list them.
>
> _____
> _____
> _____
> _____
> _____

Judging from your examination, what message do you think Paul is sending to Titus in this passage?

_____
_____
_____
_____

How can this message be applied to you?

_____
_____
_____
_____

During your introduction of Titus, you would have found out that the church Titus was leading was in Crete, and you might have noticed Paul's statement in 1:12 that Cretans are always liars, evil beasts, lazy gluttons. In fact, Paul asserts that this statement was made by one of their own prophets. An investigation of the Cretans would reveal that they were described to be a people who were so greedy that it did not matter how they got their money. Their own historians noted that the Cretans were engaged in more public and private murders than almost any other nation. Their public and private lives, including the government, was said to be one of the most treacherous and inequitable of any known people.

Knowing this can certainly help you understand why Paul would be trying to make a specific point about how the Cretans should act, and this point is partially revealed in the study of the words/phrases he repeated throughout chapters 2 and 3, which I am sure you discovered in the above exercise.

Comparison and **contrast** are two other tools used by biblical writers. They are used by the author to clarify an idea. The book of Proverbs, for example, does this consistently. You will sometimes read where a wise man does one thing, while a fool does the opposite. By contrasting the actions of the wise with the actions of the foolish, Solomon has shown us just how wise a wise man is and just how foolish a fool is.

Comparison is similar to contrast. Sometimes a comparison can be difficult to discover, but when found can be extremely helpful in gaining understanding of a passage.

In Matthew 11:29 – 30, Jesus invites us to take His yoke upon ourselves so we could learn from Him. He goes on to explain that His yoke is easy and His burden is light. What does He mean? A little investigation reveals the way yokes worked in Jesus' day. Whenever a farmer needed to train a young and inexperienced ox he would yoke him together with an older experienced ox. The older ox knew what to do and the younger ox would learn from him as he walked with him and copied everything he did. Also, the yoke could be adjusted so that the experienced ox pulled the full weight of the load. As the younger ox grew in strength and ability, the load would be gradually shifted so he pulled more of the weight each day until he was doing all the work.

Jesus is comparing His relationship with us to the relationship of two oxen. The younger ox still had to work, but the more capable ox carried the load and the responsibility. The younger ox continued to abide with the older ox until he began to develop the same ability and character as the older ox. By studying the relationship of the oxen, we can better understand our relationship with Jesus. When Jesus says His yoke is easy and His burden is light, He didn't mean there would be no work for us to do. He certainly did not mean that the bulk of our lives would be spent living easily in Christian comfort. Instead, like the younger ox, He expects us to do all the work we are able to handle. The young ox could not handle much at first, and neither can we as new and inexperienced Christians. But like the young ox, we are expected to grow in relationship to the Lord as we walk and learn from Him, just like the young ox learned from the older ox. We are also expected to grow in strength, just like the younger ox became stronger daily. In addition, the same way the young ox became increasingly able to handle more of the workload because of his increasing strength, relationship to the older ox, and familiarity with the task he has been assigned to accomplish, so we as Christians should be increasingly able to handle more Kingdom workload and responsibility because we should be growing in relationship to the Lord, strength, and familiarity with the task God has assigned to us. Comparing the relationship between the two oxen to our relationship with Christ illumines our understanding of what Jesus was trying to explain.

Comparison and contrast are similar tools and many times they will produce the same type of insights into a passage of Scripture. The difference between these two is simple. When comparing, you are learning how the two situations being compared are alike, like the yoked oxen and being yoked to Christ. When contrasting, you are learning how they differ, like the differences between the priest, the Levite, and the Samaritan in one of Jesus' parables. Once you have determined this, use the information to enhance your meaning of the passage. Try this exercise in contrast:

Examine **Luke 10: 25 – 37**.

Why is Jesus telling this parable?
_____
_____
_____

What is the difference between being a Samaritan and being a Jew?
_____
_____
_____

What is the difference in the attitudes of the three men who passed by?
_____
_____
_____

Why might their attitudes be so different?
_____
_____
_____

What cultural factors might influence their attitudes?
_____
_____
_____
_____

What religious factors might be influencing their attitudes?
_____
_____
_____
_____

What are some of the lessons Jesus is using this parable to teach?
_____
_____
_____
_____
_____

What are some of the differences between the priest, the Levite, and the Samaritan? What were their cultural or societal roles? What type of occupation might the Samaritan have been working in? Does his apparent wealth give him an unfair advantage in helping the injured traveler? Does an apparent lack of wealth of the priest and Levite excuse them from helping the injured traveler?

The road between Jerusalem and Jericho was known to be dangerous. Many were robbed while traveling that road. Can the fear of being a victim excuse the priest and Levite from being a good neighbor? Can the fear of your neighbor allow you to refuse to love them? What if they are racists? What if they are homosexual? What if they are mean? What if they just won a lawsuit against you?

After studying this parable, there are many lessons you could have learned. The fundamental lesson Jesus is teaching about loving your neighbor as yourself will find all types of applications in your circumstances at home and work. Loving neighbors has little to do with how you feel or how uncomfortable the circumstances are. It only concerns itself with meeting the need the best way you know how and are able to do. You can figure this out by contrasting, or studying the differences between the priest, the Levite, and the Samaritan.

Another practice that can facilitate your understanding of a paragraph is **translating** key words in the paragraph into their original language (Hebrew or Aramaic in the Old Testament and Greek in the New Testament). Sometimes, the words in the original language do not have an exact match in English. By reverting to the original language and finding the meaning, you will sometimes see nuances that will shed light on the meaning of a passage.

There are three words for love in Greek. *Phileo* means brotherly love. *Agape* is a sacrificial, unconditional love, while *eros* is sexual love. In John 21:15-17 the benefit of translation is made clear.

Jesus asks Peter if he loves Him. Peter responds "Yes, Lord; You know that I love You." Jesus asks again if he loves Him. Peter gives the same reply. A third time Jesus asks Peter if he loves Him. This time Peter was grieved at the Lord's question, but he makes the same reply. At first glance, this passage can be confusing. But translating the word *love* sheds a whole new light on this Scripture. Let's read it again while using the original Greek translation for the word love in this passage.

Jesus asks Peter "do you *agape* Me?" Peter replies "Yes, Lord; You know that I *phileo* You." Jesus asks again "Simon, son of John, do you *agape* Me?" Peter said "Yes, Lord; You know that I *phileo* You." Jesus asks a third time "Simon, son of John, do you *phileo* Me?" This time Peter was grieved because Jesus used the word *phileo* instead of *agape*, but he responds "Lord, You know all things; You know that I *phileo* You."

Seeing the translation brings a new understanding to this passage. Jesus wants Peter to love Him unconditionally. Peter honestly responds that the best he could do was to be Jesus' friend. Jesus accepts Peter just the way he is. Can you see how this Scripture can apply to you? The next time you begin telling the Lord how much you love Him, just be honest with Him and He will accept you exactly the way you are. When you are unable to rise to His level, He is willing and able to meet you at your level.

The rule of **context** is one of the most crucial in interpreting a passage. The truths that are seen in a paragraph do not stand alone. They are intimately related to the truths that surround it. For example, many people use Philippians 4:19 to encourage each other that God will provide for their every need. But a careful examination of that passage (vs. 10-21) will reveal the discussion of the Philippian Church who sacrificially gave to support Paul's ministry. It is because of their giving, Paul teaches, that God will provide for them. A lazy person who will not work should not expect God to give him anything based on Philippians 4:19. God is not providing for the Philippians just because they are His children; He does so because they are His faithful children who give selflessly. The lazy person needs to study 2 Thessalonians 3:6-15.

It is easy to keep things in context when studying a book in the Bible. It is a little more difficult when completing a topical study. We will discuss topical studies in a later chapter.

Finally, **cross referencing** can also be an important tool in understanding passages. Many times during your study you will encounter words or phrases that are difficult to understand (e.g., "crown of life" in James 1:12). One effective way to understand these terms is to cross reference them to other parts of Scripture. By seeing how they are used elsewhere, especially by the same author in another of his writings, we can sometimes acquire a better understanding of them.

Many Bibles have cross references in the center margin. If available, these references can be the quickest ones to use. Otherwise, a concordance can easily be used to track down words and terms. Cross references are not exhaustive, so it is always a good idea to have a concordance available anyway.

Step 5: Study the Sentences

This step is not always necessary; but if you have trouble with a paragraph, it may help to break the paragraph into sentences. This is easy to do. Just look at the punctuation in the verses to see where one sentence ends and the next one begins. By taking the paragraph one sentence at a time and analyzing it for the subject and verb and examining its phrases and clauses (along with other grammatical elements), you can improve your understanding of the paragraph you are studying.

The second paragraph of Ephesians chapter one is loaded with content. It can be difficult to grasp the message Paul is trying to send to his readers. Examining this passage sentence by sentence can help draw out its meaning. The second paragraph begins in verse 3 and runs through verse14. The first sentence reads:

> 3 Blessed be the God and Father of our Lord Jesus Christ, who has blessed us with every spiritual blessing in the heavenly places in Christ,
> 4a just as He chose us in Him before the foundation of the world, that we should be holy and blameless before Him.

This first sentence explains what God did and how He did it. He blessed us with every spiritual blessing, which Paul will use the rest of this paragraph to explain and chose us before the foundation of the world to receive those blessings. The end of this sentence tells us why He did this: so that we would be holy and blameless in love. So this sentence sets the foundation for the rest of the paragraph. After an examination of the other sentences, we are likely to notice that they will expand on what the first sentence means. Let's continue:

> 4b In love
> 5 He predestined us to adoption as sons through Jesus Christ to Himself, according to the kind intention of His will,
> 6 to the praise of the glory of His grace, which He freely bestowed on us in the Beloved.

This sentence reiterates what Paul said in the first sentence when it mentions that we were predestined to be adopted as sons. He did this because it was His will to do it. The next sentence:

> 7 In Him we have redemption through His blood, the forgiveness of our trespasses, according to the riches of His grace,
> 8a which He lavished upon us.

Here, we have redemption and forgiveness of our sins. Why? Because of the riches of His grace. How is this accomplished? Through the blood of His Son, Jesus Christ.

> 8b In all wisdom and insight
> 9 He made known to us the mystery of His will, according to His kind intention which He purposed in Him
> 10a with a view to an administration suitable to the fullness of the times, that is, the summing up of all things in Christ, things in the heavens and things upon the earth.

Paul describes in this sentence God's decision to reveal a part of His plan for humanity that had previously been hidden. He calls it the mystery of His will and defines it as an administration.

> 10b In Him
> 11 also we have obtained an inheritance, having been predestined according to His purpose who works all things after the counsel of His will,
> 12 to the end that we who were the first to hope in Christ should be to the praise of His glory.

Now, an inheritance is mentioned. This inheritance is given because of our predestination, which is mentioned in an earlier sentence as the cause of our adoption as sons.

> 13 In Him, you also, after listening to the message of truth, the gospel of your salvation – having also believed, you were sealed in Him with the Holy Spirit of promise,
> 14 who is given as a pledge of our inheritance, with a view to the redemption of God's own possession, to the praise of His glory.

Paul states here that after being saved, we were sealed in Him with the Holy Spirit. This action taken by the Holy Spirit is allowed because of our inheritance, which we have because of our adoption, which we received because of our predestination, which we were chosen for by God before the foundation of the world.

A quick examination of these sentences individually helps us understand a little more about what Paul is trying to say to his readers. You won't acquire an exhaustive understanding of what is in this paragraph, but studying the sentences will give you a head start toward reaching that goal.

It's easy to see how Paul progresses his theme when looking at the sentences. Each sentence has a structure that is nearly identical to the ones surrounding it. Let's quickly analyze each sentence.

Each sentence speaks of a gift given to us from God. It mentions why the gift was given, and the first two sentences tell us that the way we received these gifts was through the blood of Jesus Christ. The reason for the gifts, mentioned in the second, fifth, and sixth sentences is said to be for the praise of His glory.

It is interesting to see how the gifts we have in the last sentences are dependent upon the gift in the second sentence, and how all the gifts mentioned combine to include all spiritual blessings. In other words, Paul says in the first sentence that God chose to bless us with every spiritual blessing in the heavenly places. The first blessing he describes is our predestination. The predestination allows us to be adopted as sons. We become members of God's family because He adopted us. Because we are now a part of His family, we can receive redemption, forgiveness of our sins (sentence three), a new understanding of His plans for the Church (sentence four), an inheritance (sentence five), and sealing with the Holy Spirit (sentence six).

It is also important to notice that He did this so that we would be holy and blameless (sentence one), and that He would be praised (sentences two, five, and six). The extra bonus we receive, mentioned in sentences two and three, is an outpouring of His grace upon us.

So it is clear that Paul begins in the first sentence by mentioning God's decision to make us a part of His family and to bestow upon us all the spiritual blessings we would ever need, and he

	v.3	v.4	v.7	v.8	v.10	v.13
	Blessed be God the Father	In love	In Him	In wisdom and insight	In Him	In Him
Gift	Every spiritual blessing in the heavenly places	Predestined to adoption as sons	Redemption: the forgiveness of sins	Revelation of the mystery	Inheritance	Sealed with the Holy Spirit
Because of		His kind intention	The riches of His grace	His kind intention	Our predestination	Our inheritance
Method	His choosing us	Through Jesus	Jesus' blood			
Why?	That we should be holy and blameless	To the praise of His glory			To the praise of His glory	To the praise of His glory
Bonus		Grace is freely bestowed on us	Grace is lavished upon us			

spends the remainder of this paragraph describing why He did it, what exactly the spiritual blessings include, how it was accomplished, and what He expects to see from us because of what He did. If you were studying Ephesians and had completed an overview of the book, you might have realized by now that the remainder of Ephesians is a more detailed explanation of the concepts in this paragraph.

This cursory approach to the sentences is by no means exhaustive. All of this information can be gathered by taking a quick glance at each sentence. Going into further detail might mean using your junior high grammar skills to diagram the sentences. You can look for subjects, verbs, clauses, objects, phrases, adjectives, etc. to try to understand more about each sentence. You could also learn Greek and read it in its original language to learn more about Paul's exact message. If you balk at learning Greek, you can use your study tools to define some of the words in this passage in order to amplify their meaning. In addition, since there is a lot of material in Scripture written by Paul, you can use the cross references in your study bible to see where and how he might have used the same terms or concepts in some of his other writings. Understanding what he means by being holy and blameless, or by being predestined, for example, can help you understand what he means by those words or phrases when he uses them here.

Step 6: Complete a Chart of the Book

We mentioned making a chart following the overview stage of study. If you chose to make a chart, this is where you would refine it and add details. It would probably be easier to achieve this one step at a time as you work your way through the book.

Remember, this step is helpful, but optional. Several elements that can be charted are historical elements, biographical elements, geographical elements, doctrinal elements, chronological elements, logical elements, topical elements, and key words. Adding details to your chart will enhance it and make it more useful.

Your chart will become a visual representation of your study. In order to keep it from becoming too detailed, many students will stop building their charts once they complete their overview.

Refocus

Remember, we study Scripture to intensify our relationship with our Lord Jesus Christ. It can be addicting to search for and acquire information about God by studying His word. You can easily become a know-it-all and impress others with your biblical knowledge. It is also easy to become more addicted to the knowledge than to Jesus Christ. A way to prevent that is to remember the lessons from chapter two, when we talked about study being a form of worship.

It also will help to remember to constantly communicate with the Lord while studying. Communication is the tool that is used to build relationships. Without it, a relationship, no matter what kind, will falter and die. Your relationship with God is no different. Communication is necessary for a healthy and productive relationship with the Father.

Your study of His word should be for the purpose of building that relationship. Your study should not begin with the sole seeking of knowledge, nor should it end with the acquisition of information. Rather, your study should begin with an intense desire to know God and it should end with you applying the information you find to your life.

But communication is a two-way street. God speaks to us through His word; but if we were unable to talk back, the relationship would still die. Therefore, it is essential that you pray. Prayer is the way we can talk to God. Your study of His word should be surrounded by prayer. You should pray to understand His word before you even begin; and throughout your study, you should continually pray for advice on how to apply things you are learning or for an understanding of a passage you are struggling with. Anytime your study causes you to react, you usually need to either praise God or ask for His forgiveness, and the only way you can do those things is through prayer.

Conclusion

There will never be a conclusion to your study. When you complete the study of the book you have chosen, you might find it easier choose another book written by the same author and study it. When you complete the study of the entire author's work, you can continue in the section in which you began. After finishing the section, choose another section until every section in the testament in completed. Then begin in the other testament and start over. When you finish the Bible, start over. Here is an example of the suggested order of study of the New Testament:

1. Gospels
    A. Matthew
    B. Mark
    C. Luke
    D. Acts
    E. John
    F. 1, 2 & 3 John
    G. Revelation
2. History
    A. Acts
    B. Luke
3. Pauline Epistles
    A. Romans
    B. 1 & 2 Corinthians
    C. Galatians
    D. Ephesians
    E. Philippians
    F. Colossians
    G. 1 & 2 Thessalonians
    H. 1 & 2 Timothy
    I. Titus
    J. Philemon
4. General Epistles
    A. Hebrews
    B. James
    C. 1 & 2 Peter
    D. 1, 2 & 3 John
    E. John
    F. Revelation
    G. Jude

> 5. Prophecy
>   A. Revelation
>   B. John
>   C. 1, 2 & 3 John

This book is intended to provide a framework for doing Bible study. You may not do your studies exactly as specified here; but hopefully you will find practices in this book that you can use as a foundation for building your relationship with God by intensifying your communication with Him.

It is also important to mention that the methods described so far are not as easy to apply to different types of Scripture. Studying books that are poetic, like Psalms or Proverbs, or historical, like the Chronicles, can be tough. Even narratives like Ruth and Esther can be difficult. But the basic reason for studying, relationship, and the method we used can be applied to all of Scripture. In chapter two, we discovered that Bible study is worship. Well, studying Chronicles is just as much worship as studying Ephesians. An introduction of Chronicles can be done to get a general idea of the book's background and an overview can give a good understanding of the contents. Studying the paragraphs can be trickier because they might not build upon each other like they do in didactic writings, but the paragraphs and the sentences that compose them are the smallest components of a book, and the best way to discover the details of the book is to study it at its most fundamental level. Studying this way still creates conversation with God, which still builds relationship.

Again, this is a framework for doing Bible study. You might not perform your studies exactly as prescribed here, but I pray that you can use the practices here to grow your relationship with the Lord.

5: Completing a Topical Study

There is another type of Bible study: the topical method. Like the name suggests, this method is useful for studying general topics in Scripture. For example, if you wanted to understand what the Bible teaches about controlling your anger, you would not be able to study one passage in the Bible to learn everything you need to know. You would need to search all of Scripture to gain a complete understanding of anger. You would look at the different facets of anger: its causes, its solution, its source, its effect on you, its effect on your relationships, the consequences of ignoring it, etc. The process of finding and assimilating this information is called **topical Bible study**.

Topical studies can become very broad and academic. It is easy to lose focus during these studies. The chosen topic will almost always lead to subtopics, which can draw the student into a rabbit hole that spirals continually downward. If the study is designed to be academic, the downward spiral might actually be a good thing. In other words, a student who is making a study in order to present a paper, or prepare a sermon, or complete a seminary assignment will most likely need to examine his topic from multiple angles. He will need to present a thorough analysis of the topic. To accomplish this, he will investigate as many of the subtopics as possible.

Most who begin a topical study are not trying to meet an academic requirement. Their need is more personal and they will seek information about a topic so they can understand which course of action they should take. They might also need to be able to form a biblical opinion about a cultural issue so that they can speak intelligently about it to others. These types of topical studies are usually narrower than the academic topical study. For example, someone might need to study gambling because either they or someone they know has an issue in this area. The personal study might focus on a solution to a gambling problem. It could address the objective steps needed to quit gambling as well as where to go for strength to actually carry out the steps. The academic study could delve into the causes of gambling addictions, the effects on the gambler and others, the consequences of their problem and the theological explanation of why it is sin. The person caught in gambling might care less about the theological explanation of the sin, he only wants to be rid of it in his life. The effect of gambling on him and others is probably something he knows too well. He does not need a Bible study to explain that to him.

Becoming too academic is only one problem that is inherent in topical studies. Another problem that is difficult to avoid is violating the rule of context. We spoke about this in the previous chapter when we discussed regular book studies and concluded that it is vitally important to study your Scripture in its surrounding context. This is also important in topical studies. The nature of topical studies is to scramble through Scripture pulling out various verses from all sorts of books. It's easy to compile a list of verses and examine them at face value. But this is a dangerous practice. Let's re-examine the passage we used as an example earlier, Philippians chapter 4. If you were doing a topical study about God being your source, or supplier, you would undoubtedly come across Philippians 4:19, and you would be tempted to jump and shout because of this promise. It is awfully tempting to take this verse at face value, sit back and relax, and know that God will give you anything you ever need. Until, you decide to read the entire passage (vs 15-20). Applying the rule of context show you that the reason God supplied all the Philippians' needs is because they selflessly gave so that the needs of others were met. Well this is a whole different story. Now, instead of sitting back and believing you are entitled to all sorts of good stuff, you realize that God's supply is in response to your sacrificial giving. This truth forces you to examine your giving to others. Do you tithe? Do you give offerings? Are you involved in any way in helping meet the needs of others? If the answer to any of these questions is no, the passage in Philippians might be instructing you to be more sacrificial and less selfish in your giving. Obviously, you would combine the truth here with the truths about your topic in other parts of Scripture, and we will talk about that soon, but pulling Philippians 4:19 out of context would have led to an improper conclusion about the topic you are studying. If that happens, you will miss the entire point of a topical study, which is to apply truths to problem areas of your life so that you grow closer in relationship to the Lord Jesus Christ.

Obviously, the topical study can be as narrow or as wide as it is needed to be. The key for someone making a personal topical study is to avoid getting carried away by the temptation to study purely for information. We have spoken much about the goal of Bible study being relationship. A personal topical study enhances our relationship with the Lord in the sense that it is done to address problem areas in our lives. If a study begins with the attempt to eradicate a sin so that we can please God, but ends with a broad theological treatise without much action, then the study has not achieved its purpose.

The final and ultimate challenge of a personal study is to end it with an action plan to put in place. During election season, it would be a good idea to know how to vote. Completing a study on the issues will only help you please God if you actually vote the way Scripture leads you to vote. Otherwise, your study has become academic and may not help you build a stronger relationship to the Lord.

Step 1: Choose a Topic

There are several factors which may influence your decision about choosing a topic. You may want to study an issue you are having a problem overcoming. Or you may need to study a topic you will be speaking about to a group of people. Or someone you know may need you to explain an issue to them that you are not familiar with. Whatever the reason, you must begin by choosing a topic to study.

Step 2: List Key Words, Phrases, People, Places, and Scriptures

After you have decided, you will need to make a list of the key words or phrases that are associated with your topic. Sometimes, there will be key people, places or events that you can use to gather information about your topic. For example, if you wanted to study humility, your list may resemble that of the example given in the table below.

Key Words or Phrases	Key People	Key Scriptures
Humble	Moses	Daniel 4
Exalt	Job	Job 40
Obedience	Nebuchadnezzar	Proverbs 16
Haughty	Naaman	
Pride	Jesus	

Step 3: Use Study Tools to Find Key Information

There are several resources that can be used to identify the location of your key words in the Bible. The most useful of these is the **concordance**. This tool is valuable because it will help you get a fast start. The concordance is a list of words found in the Bible. Next to the word, there will be a scripture reference so you will know where to look for that word. You might be able to find all the words you need in a concordance, but if you cannot, you will need to use an **exhaustive concordance**. This reference will list every word in the Bible, so that whatever topic you are investigating, you will find the key words on your list.

Another resource is a **topical index** or **topical bible**. This is not an exhaustive resource in that it does not list every reference in Scripture to the topics it gives information about. The characteristic of this resource that makes it useful is the identification of new key words. If you cannot think of any key words or phrases to use in your research of your topic, the topical index can sometimes provide some for you.

Cross references are also good resources. They are found in the center margin of most study bibles. When you begin looking at the verses which deal with your topic, a study bible may cross reference a particular word or phrase to other places in the Bible. If these cross-referenced words or phrases match your key words or phrases, then you may have found a new source of information concerning your topic.

Whenever new key words are found, you can use the concordance to search them out in the Bible. You can also use the concordance to find key scriptures. You might be able to quote a passage of Scripture loosely, and you might know it's found somewhere in the Gospels, but if you can remember any identifying words from that passage, you might be able to look them up in the concordance and find the passage you need. For example, you might decide to study the topic of judging others. You have always heard it said "the Bible says not to judge", but you don't know if it really says that, and if it does, where would you find it? A quick look in a concordance will lead you to Matthew 7:1. From there, the cross references can lead you to other similar verses and passages.

There are other resources available. Books on your topic have probably been written and if they have, you will usually find them in a local bookstore. Also, you may know someone who is an authority on your topic and you can go to them for information. Also, as mentioned in an earlier chapter, there are always online resources available.

Step 4: Gather Information

After finding out where to go for information, go get it! You have found out where your key words, people, and scriptures are found in the Bible; the next step is to look at the references and gather all of the information you can. You will need to do this by utilizing the skills you developed in the Bible study method that is described in the previous chapter.

Again, it is important to remember to study your scriptures in the context of the passages where they are found. Otherwise, your study could lead to false information. We discussed this earlier; to re-iterate, let's expand on an example we used earlier. How many times have you heard someone say "the Bible says not to judge"? If you read Matthew 7:1, it would seem to be a correct statement. However, the paragraph only begins in verse 1. It ends in verse 5. Studying the entire paragraph reveals the truth about judging, which is that we need to be careful about how we judge. Judging is mandatory, but judging carelessly is dangerous. If you only pay attention to verse 1, you would have an incorrect view of the biblical teaching on judging. Someone studying judging might look at Matthew 7:1 and read "Do not judge lest you be judged" and conclude that he is condemning judging. But a closer examination of that entire paragraph (verses 1-5) reveals Matthew's true message, which is to judge others, but do it cautiously.

As mentioned above, a student making a topical study must be careful to apply the Bible study skills discussed in chapter four to the topical study as well. Most topical studies, however, can be completed without book introductions and overviews. Most of the time, using the skills developed in your study of paragraphs will be sufficient.

Step 5: Study the Information

Once you have gathered facts and observations on your topic, you will need to assimilate the information into a useable format. This process will cause you to begin dividing your topic into several areas. For example, if you were studying humility, you may look at your information and notice that sometimes the Bible talks about how to obtain humility. Or you may notice that God's actions and attitude towards a man who has no humility are discussed. These different areas of focus will become subtopics, and these subtopics will allow you to have a thorough understanding of your topic. However, as we have discussed, it is important to be careful about exploring too many subtopics, especially if your study is personal, not academic.

Many times, topical studies are quick and potent. They certainly will not take as long as a regular Bible book study, and they are useful for learning God's perspective on everything that affects our lives as Christians. Many times, these studies can be completed in a couple of hours, or less. But they are just as likely to take a long time, depending on the topic.

Let's use our example on judging as a practice exercise.

List all the key people, words, phrases, or scriptures you can think of

_____

_____

_____

_____

Use the topical index or concordance to find as many scripture references for your key words, people, etc. as you can

_____
_____
_____
_____
_____
_____

Begin by examining the scripture passages you have found

_____
_____
_____
_____
_____
_____

Try to use the scripture passages you are studying to think of more key people, words, phrases, or scriptures. List them here as you think of them. Try using the cross references from the passage you are studying.

_____
_____
_____
_____
_____
_____

Look up the new words, etc. you have thought of. List the new scriptures you want to examine here.

_____
_____
_____
_____
_____
_____

Study the new passages. Note some of your findings here

_____
_____
_____
_____
_____
_____

List any subtopics about judging that you might have thought of or that your study so far has shown you

_____
_____
_____
_____
_____
_____
_____

Which are relevant to what you need to know? Which are irrelevant? Determine a path of your study by ignoring the subtopics of judging that do not interest you or are not useful to you

_____

_____

_____

_____

_____

_____

Continue your study and list the lessons you have learned here

_____

_____

_____

_____

_____

_____

How will you apply these lessons?

_____

_____

_____

_____

_____

_____

Hopefully, this exercise will give you an idea of how a topical study works. As you begin studying the passages you find, you will inevitably think of new passages, people, or situations that will help expand your study. Maybe there's a situation you can remember where a person was judged. Were they judged for their sin or for their preferences? In your study, did you determine that there was even a difference between judging sin and judging preferences?

These are the types of questions that might arise and can lead you into an endless spiral of more questions, more investigation, more findings, and on and on until you bury yourself beneath an unmanageable pile of facts, details, thoughts, opinions, and conclusions that may or may not even mean anything to your study. It's possible that you won't even be able to use much of the information that you gathered, especially if your study is personal. Filtering out information that will not help you decide what to do about your specific situation is one of the most difficult practices to master in topical studies.

Refocus

Remember, study is a relationship building exercise. Like a book study, a topical study will yield a lot of information. Accumulating facts can be addictive, but remember that building relationship will produce facts, but accumulating facts will not necessarily produce relationship. If you are making a personal topical study, you still want to see your relationship to Christ grow through your efforts. Studying a book of the Bible will grow your relationship as you engage the Scripture in meditation and prayer. Topical studies appear to be more academic and intent on information gathering than building relationship, and this is probably true if your study is academic, rather than personal. But remember that a personal topical study is probably needed to address a personal issue, possibly one that is creating a struggle in you. When this is the case, and you treat your study as worship, and you are honest with the Lord about wanting to hear from Him about your topic, you will grow closer as He guides you through your study, and the closeness will increase as you apply what you learn to how you live.

Relationship is the primary goal of Bible study, but if you do not apply the principles you learn, it won't be long before the relationship begins to suffer. Application is important enough to discuss it separately, and we will do that in the following chapter.

6: Applying God's Word

Well, what good does all of this studying do? Sure, by applying the process described in the previous chapters you will learn a great deal about the Bible's contents, but throughout this book we have discussed the desire to increase relationship with the Lord. In fact, we have shown some of the benefits of getting and remaining connected to Christ. This connection is achieved by communicating with the Lord through study and prayer, but how is it maintained? All of us know that relationships can begin well and end poorly. If you and your business partner begin a business and determine that you would build it by incorporating certain standards and practices, you would probably get off to a strong start. But if one of you decided not to abide by the agreed upon practices, the relationship would eventually sour. You might know a lot about your business, but if you don't obey the practices needed to make the business grow and thrive, your knowledge would be useless. Knowing is important, but refusing to use what you know will limit your business growth.

In the same way, the start to a relationship with Christ can be exciting. You are hearing Him speak clearly to you from Scripture, maybe for the first time ever. You are beginning to understand how your pastor and other great Bible teachers can come up with some of the teachings they express to their audiences. After a while, you begin to realize that maybe you are not learning as much as you were when you began. Or maybe you don't have that same exciting feeling you used to when it was time to open your Bible. Or perhaps that exciting feeling left you when it was time to do the things God was saying you need to do. You, like Moses and Jonah, might not want to obey God because He is telling you to do something you don't want to do. Perhaps obeying would be too hard, or the solution to your troubles sounds a little strange and it doesn't make sense to you. It's like when God says that to help resolve your financial issues, you should give more money away. Really? Why would you do that? It doesn't make sense.

The way to keep your relationship growing is to just apply the Word the way God instructs you to do it. Just like the way to keep your business growing is to practice the things you learn about the business, even when it doesn't always make sense. If you had trouble applying your business principles you would get help. For example, you would probably hire an accountant to help with the financial strategies and practices to help your business grow. Your relationship with Christ is the same. You will, at times, need someone to help you do what you need to do. They will help you form strategies for obedience and develop habits that will make it possible and increasingly easier to obey God's Word. The key is to obey God. If you do, you will see you and your life change and your relationship will continue to grow.

In 2 Kings 5, there is a story of someone who responded to God's instructions the same way many of us respond to His Word. Let's look at Naaman the Syrian.

> 1 Now Naaman, captain of the army of the king of Aram, was a great man with his master, and highly respected, because by him the LORD had given victory to Aram. The man was also a valiant warrior, *but he was* a leper.
>
> 2 Now the Arameans had gone out in bands and had taken captive a little girl from the land of Israel; and she waited on Naaman's wife.
>
> 3 She said to her mistress, "I wish that my master were with the prophet who is in Samaria! Then he would cure him of his leprosy."
>
> 4 Naaman went in and told his master, saying, "Thus and thus spoke the girl who is from the land of Israel."
>
> 5 Then the king of Aram said, "Go now, and I will send a letter to the king of Israel." He departed and took with him ten talents of silver and six thousand *shekels* of gold and ten changes of clothes.

Naaman is described to be a great man who was accomplished in battle. Because the Lord had given him numerous victories, he was considered to be a formidable and valiant warrior. His problem was that he had leprosy. This was a disease that would soon isolate Naaman and prevent him from leading the Aramean military forces. However, Naaman's wife was served by an Israelite girl who knew of the prophet Elisha who could possibly heal Naaman from his leprosy. The problem was that she didn't say the prophet *could possibly* heal Naaman, but that he *would* heal him. So the King of Aram sent Naaman to the Israelite King commanding him to heal Naaman of his leprosy.

Of course, the King can't cure leprosy and he predictably becomes upset, thinking that the King of Aram is setting him up. He figures that if he doesn't comply with the order to heal Naaman, it would give Aram an excuse to act against Israel.

> 6 He brought the letter to the king of Israel, saying, "And now as this letter comes to you, behold, I have sent Naaman my servant to you, that you may cure him of his leprosy."
>
> 7 When the king of Israel read the letter, he tore his clothes and said, "Am I God, to kill and to make alive, that this man is sending *word* to me to cure a man of his leprosy? But consider now, and see how he is seeking a quarrel against me."
>
> 8 It happened when Elisha the man of God heard that the king of Israel had torn his clothes, that he sent *word* to the king, saying, "Why have you torn your clothes? Now let him come to me, and he shall know that there is a prophet in Israel."

> 9 So Naaman came with his horses and his chariots and stood at the doorway of the house of Elisha.
>
> 10 Elisha sent a messenger to him, saying, "Go and wash in the Jordan seven times, and your flesh will be restored to you and *you will* be clean."

Naaman was given specific instructions by the man of God, but he didn't like what he heard. He had his own idea about how this meeting would go. When the instructions failed to meet his expectations, he became furious.

> 11 But Naaman was furious and went away and said, "Behold, I thought, 'He will surely come out to me and stand and call on the name of the LORD his God, and wave his hand over the place and cure the leper.'
>
> 12 Are not Abanah and Pharpar, the rivers of Damascus, better than all the waters of Israel? Could I not wash in them and be clean?" So he turned and went away in a rage.

The prophet's instructions made no sense to Naaman. It wasn't logical that a dirty river like the Jordan would clean better than a cleaner river like the ones in Damascus. He obviously knew a better way to solve his leprosy than Elisha. The problem is that none of his efforts provided the desired solution in the past. How many times must he have bathed in Damascus' rivers only to emerge with the same leprosy he had when he went in? It's a good thing his servants had a better perspective on the situation.

> [13] Then his servants came near and spoke to him and said, "My father, had the prophet told you *to do some* great thing, would you not have done *it*? How much more *then*, when he says to you, 'Wash, and be clean'?"

Naaman's servants used common sense to convince Naaman to re-think his rejection of Elisha's instructions. After all, they had come a long way to try something; why not do something goofy, just in case it worked? And the servants were right. If Elisha had told Naaman to climb Mt. Everest and bring back the lower left petal of a flower that only grew at the summit during the third week in November during odd numbered years, he would have done it. How much more should he have done something simple, like take a bath in the river?

> [14] So he went down and dipped *himself* seven times in the Jordan, according to the word of the man of God; and his flesh was restored like the flesh of a little child and he was clean.

Imagine Naaman's shock when he discovered that his skin was as fresh as a child's. He must have been both surprised and exuberant at his newfound health. He was definitely convinced that God is real and was grateful over what He had done.

> 15 When he returned to the man of God with all his company, and came and stood before him, he said, "Behold now, I know that there is no God in all the earth, but in Israel; so please take a present from your servant now."

Naaman understood now just how capable God is. He never would have known God's power if he had refused to apply His instructions to his life.

Obviously, the optimal behavior from Naaman would have been to tell the prophet "of course I'll bathe seven times in the river, since God has commanded it! I would never ignore His instructions or disobey His commands!" But that rarely happens. The truth is that all of us have trouble doing what God says, and we experience this trouble more often than we care to admit. How did Naaman move from anger to application? What lessons can we learn from his experience?

Like many of us, when Naaman came to hear God's solution, he had a preconceived notion about the type of solution to expect. We do this all the time. We ask God to help us with our financial trouble and our expectation is that He will send a job promotion, or a windfall of some sort. When He decides to take away a house or a car, or reject your daughter's acceptance into Yale, we can become angry or confused. You didn't expect God to solve your problem that way. He was supposed to do what *you* wanted Him to do, because you obviously know how to resolve your money issues better than God. Instead of a cash windfall or a new job, God might be saying "sell the house and move into something smaller", or "send your daughter to community college for two years, then she can go to Yale". When this happens, would you respond the way Naaman did? Would you angrily pout about His unwanted and unorthodox solution to your problem?

Here is lesson number one about applying God's word to your life: don't always expect Him to tell you what you *want* to hear. He rarely solves problems the way we would, and He probably never solves them for the same reasons we think He does. How many times has He worked in our lives in inexplicable ways only for us to discover, maybe even years later, exactly what He was doing and why He chose the path for us that He did.

Lesson two about application of the Word of God: don't always expect Him to tell you what you *expect* to hear. Naaman thought God would magically solve his problem. He might not have cared how his leprosy was healed, but he sure had some expectations. He thought Elisha would emerge and do a magic trick and heal his leprosy. He didn't plan on expending any effort in his quest for clean skin. But God's actual instruction was a little confusing. How strange must Joshua have felt when God told him to march his army around Jericho once a day for six days, and then march around it seven times on the seventh day? Despite what he might have been thinking, he did it without question and on the seventh day the walls fell. This probably was not the plan Joshua was expecting to hear, but he obeyed, even though the instructions were unusual. I'm pretty sure he didn't storm off, whining about how God decided to solve this problem. Joshua certainly had the advantage over Naaman because he had witnessed some of God's strange solutions before. After seeing the plagues God brought against Egypt and the parting of the Red Sea, along with raining manna from Heaven and all the other ways God provided and protected during their forty-year trek through the wilderness, it was easier for Joshua to accept God's plan for Jericho than it must have been for Naaman to accept God's solution for his leprosy.

Naaman had no such experiences. He had no history with God, so there was no way for him to understand that God will sometimes develop strange ways of getting His work done. This leads to lesson three in applying God's Word: have people in your life who can straighten you out when you get bent out of shape. If Naaman's servants had not been there to calm him down and speak some wisdom into his situation, he might have returned to Aram with leprosy. Furthermore, the king of Aram might have used the situation to start a new quarrel with Israel. When God is telling you something about your life that you don't want to hear, you should listen to people who have been in your shoes before. Or even if they haven't, they might have a clearer, less emotional perspective on your situation. Naaman's servants did not have leprosy. They probably could have cared less about whether he was ever healed of his. Their detachment from Naaman's circumstance allowed them to have an objective view of the instruction given to him by Elisha.

Lesson four: your attitude is irrelevant. Don't worry about how you feel about God's instruction. And certainly don't try to lie to Him about what you're feeling. He already knows anyway if you're skeptical, or even angry about what He's telling you to do. Moses certainly didn't want to go to Egypt, and he told God he didn't want to go. I'm pretty sure Jonah didn't want to go to Nineveh, and Gideon was certainly a little afraid to fight against Midian. He was unsure of his ability and asked for a sign from God at least three times so that he could be sure that God wanted him to complete this great task. The important thing is that all three of these men did what they were told, even though Jonah had to be compelled to obey. In the same way,

Naaman had an attitude after receiving his instructions, but he did it anyway. He didn't lie and pretend that he thought bathing in the Jordan was a great idea, hoping to fool God into thinking the he was excited to obey. He was honest about what he thought and felt. But he did it anyway, with the help of some good advice from his servants.

And don't think that you must get your attitude right before you embark on God's plan. God is not as concerned with your attitude as He is with your obedience. Besides, He understands that if you keep following His Word, your attitude will change. This leads to lesson five: keep track of your history with God. It will make it easier to obey in the future and lead you to accept difficult challenges as they arise in your life. Moses had a problem going to Egypt until God began sending plagues. After obeying and seeing what God could and would do, I'm sure Moses' attitude began to reform itself. By the time Moses died, he was considered by God to be His friend.

Think about David. In 1 Samuel 17:34-37, David was about to embark on a challenge that all of Israel, including the king, was afraid to tackle: he was going to fight Goliath. When Saul tried to talk him out of it, David informed Saul that he knew he would defeat Goliath because he had accomplished similar feats in the past. David remembered his history with God. God helped him defeat lions and bears when they were attacking his sheep. David knew, because he had seen it, that if God would deliver him from powerful animals for the sake of a few sheep, He would certainly deliver him from the hand of Goliath for the sake of all of Israel. David had no doubts about what God could and would do because his history with God gave him a platform of confidence. He knew he could achieve this impossible task because he had confidence in God. Notice that no one asked David to fight Goliath. He wasn't coerced into it, shamed into it, and he didn't draw the short straw. He confidently volunteered for it. We spoke about Joshua earlier in this chapter who was in the same position. He had seen many deliverances from God. Because of what he knew about God, he had no trouble when it came time to apply some of God's unusual solutions to Israel's problems, like walking around Jericho every day until it was time for it to fall.

If you obey God, despite having a bad attitude, you will soon experience enough of God to change your attitude. After that, you will have less of a problem obediently applying His Word. Then, as you continue to build a history with God, you can even find yourself accepting difficult challenges, knowing you can achieve them because your history tells you that God can do anything through you, just like He did with David.

Growing in relationship is a slow process. But it will slow to a crawl if you refuse to apply the instruction God gives from His Word. This is no different than building a relationship with a person. I used to be a technician working on office equipment. The techs in our workgroup would sometimes need help determining the cause of particularly troubling issues we would sometimes have on our customers' equipment. There was one tech in our group who was unusually good at solving difficult problems. I had a habit of going to him for help when I was having trouble. After a while, I noticed that he was reluctant to share any possible solutions with me. When I asked why his attitude toward me changed, he told me that whenever he suggested a solution to my equipment problems, I would never apply them. I would usually comment on how it wouldn't work and then continue to try to figure it out myself. He finally decided that since I wasn't going to take his advice anyway, why even bother to share it? I never realized I was doing that, but if I was ignoring his advice, he was absolutely right to stop sharing it with me.

In the same way, why would God continue to give you instruction if you constantly refused to listen to Him? In James 1:5-6, James says that if you ask God for help with a trial you're having, He would not even give you instructions if He knows you are double-minded or unsure if you are going to do what He says. Think of how badly this can damage your relationship if you are talking to God, but He is refusing to respond. One sided conversations do not build relationships. In fact, they are not even conversations. Applying God's Word to life is essential for getting and staying connected to Christ.

7: What's Next?

As I promised, this is a fundamental book on Bible study. The principles explained in the previous chapters will be useful, if they are applied diligently. But fundamental principles are designed to be a foundation upon which to build. You will find out, if you don't already know, that there is so much more to Bible study than what is in this book. The additional techniques and practices you learn in the future will be added to the foundation you will build as you begin to practice these principles.

If you asked anyone what the general theme of the Bible is, you would get a different answer from each individual. Some would say the Bible is about love, others would say it's about mercy. Forgiveness is another popular answer, and so is grace.

If you asked me to define the general theme of Scripture, I would tell you that it is about redemption. The Bible is about taking man from where he is, in his sinful and fallen state, and returning him to where he was originally intended to be. The other answers mentioned are tools that God uses to redeem men. He will apply His love, mercy, grace, forgiveness and other attributes toward us in order to achieve His divine plan of redeeming us. In this plan He has tried to relate to man in different ways during different times. He tried creating us in innocence, but we messed that up in the Garden of Eden. He tried other ways, like giving the Law, but we couldn't keep it properly. After all of His attempts to make us right with Him, He decided to send His Son, Jesus Christ to die for our sins. Accepting Christ as our Lord launches us into a relationship that, if cultivated properly, will motivate and strengthen us to keep His Word and promote His Kingdom.

Building that relationship has been a common theme throughout this book because it forms the foundation that allows us to build useful and productive lives for God's Kingdom. Bible study for the purpose of maximizing that relationship is a key to becoming and remaining connected to Christ, our Savior. It is this connection to Christ that transforms us and motivates us to do His will. It strengthens us so that we can bear fruit for the Kingdom. We spoke earlier about that when we examined John 15. We mentioned how the word abide is found ten times in that passage. That passage also explains the benefits of abiding in Christ. Bible study gets us in the habit of abiding in Christ so that we can tap into the strength that flows through that vine and into us so that we can be productive for His Kingdom.

It is for this reason that I believe relationship to be the primary reason for studying the Scriptures. We talked earlier, in chapter one, about other reasons to study Scripture. All those reasons are valid, but they center on knowing more about God rather than knowing God personally. Knowing God by experiencing Him and being connected to Him is more useful to the Christian. Even if your primary concern is to know more about the Bible intellectually, a relationship will bring that knowledge. Just like getting to know a person. You can interview them or read their autobiography, or you can become friends with them. Which is better? With friendship, you'll still get the information that you would get from the interview or the autobiography, but you would add relationship that will cause you to care about the person. That caring attitude would drive you to seek the best interest of the person who has become your friend. It is important to understand that relationship increases knowledge, but knowledge does not necessarily increase relationship.

So what's next? The fact that this is a fundamental, or beginners, Bible study method has, prayerfully, been driven home. So the next step is to apply the method in order to cultivate a relationship with Christ. Taking this step will certainly build in you a desire to dig deeper. Doing so will require you to develop abilities or practices that are not thoroughly covered in this book. I mentioned in chapter one that I usually encourage my students to take other Bible study courses, and I'm encouraging you to do the same. Other courses can instruct you on the differences on studying different types of literature, or on the basic hermeneutic principles used to dig into the Word of God. It is true that the method covered in this book can be applied to all the types of literature in the Bible and it does use many of the hermeneutic principles that seminarians and Bible study experts live by, but this book does not exhaustively explain either of those processes.

Relationship is the foundation of Bible study, but all foundations exist to have something built upon them. For the student, knowledge is what will come next. As I mentioned, relationship will bring knowledge. The closer you grow to your friend, coworker, or mate, the more you will know about them. Your relationship forms the foundation, and as the relationship grows deeper, the knowledge grows stronger. Remember in chapter one, we discovered that knowledge was one of the reasons for studying the Bible? The Bible is not studied just for the sake of knowing more stuff about its contents, but when it is added to relationship it is more useful to the Christian.

The writer of Hebrews chastises his readers in 5:11-14 because instead of growing toward maturity, they are still stuck on understanding the elementary principles of God's Word. They are like newborn babes, not like the adults they should have already grown up to be. Obviously, we are expected to grow. Just like a baby grows to adulthood, so should a new Christian grow to spiritual maturity. As a baby grows, its diet changes from milk to solid food to adult food because it is growing and able to increasingly handle a more complex diet. In the same way, a Christian should see their intake of Scripture develop from elementary principles to more complex truths as they grow toward maturity.

The next step after building relationship is to grow in knowledge, not instead of relationship, but in conjunction with it. To do that, it is a good idea to take other Bible study courses so you can learn to engage Scripture with some more advanced tools at your disposal. Please understand, I am not saying that you can't grow in knowledge using what is in this book as much as you can if you had more tools at your disposal. I am saying that it is easier to grow in knowledge if you use those tools. You can build a house with hammer and nails, but wouldn't it be easier if you used a nail gun?

You will find that some of the tools, like the use of commentaries, that I do not suggest using when studying for relationship, might be acceptable when studying for knowledge.

After growing in knowledge, your next step is to become a mentor and disciple others. In the same passage in Hebrews, Paul states that his readers should be teachers of Scripture by now. They ought to be able to transfer what they know to others who are still developing in the faith. The process they experienced should develop maturity in them. They should be stronger, wiser, and more intelligent Christians because they applied the lessons they learned from their study of Scripture to their lives.

In the introduction, we defined the Bible study method in this book as Bible Study 001. The next steps described in the above sections should move you toward Bible Study 101, and then on to Bible Study 201, and on, and on, and on.

My prayer for you is for you to experience Colossians 1:9-12, and keep in mind that the Greek word for knowledge in both cases in this passage is *epignosis*:

> For this reason also, since the day we heard of it, we have not ceased to pray for you and to ask that you may be filled with the knowledge of His will in all spiritual wisdom and understanding, so that you will walk in a manner worthy of the Lord, to please Him in all respects, bearing fruit in every good work and increasing in the knowledge of God; strengthened with all power, according to His glorious might, for the attaining of all steadfastness and patience; joyously

giving thanks to the Father, who has qualified us to share in the inheritance of the saints in light.

www.ingramcontent.com/pod-product-compliance
Ingram Content Group UK Ltd.
Pitfield, Milton Keynes, MK11 3LW, UK
UKHW021310180426
11947UKWH00015B/1130